Hidden Corners
of the
Mid-Atlantic
States

Hidden Corners of the Mid-Atlantic States

Eastern Pennsylvania, New Jersey,
Virginia, Maryland and Delaware

written and illustrated by
David Yeadon

Funk & Wagnalls
New York

Other books written and illustrated by David Yeadon

Exploring Small Towns of Southern California
Exploring Small Towns of Northern California
Hidden Restaurants of Southern California
Hidden Restaurants of Northern California
Wine Tasting in California
Sumptuous Indulgence on a Shoestring—a cookbook
The New York Book of Bars, Pubs and Taverns
When the Earth Was Young: A Study of American Indian Songs
Nooks and Crannies of New York City
Hidden Corners of New England

Copyright © 1977 by David Yeadon

Designed by David Yeadon

Manufactured in the United States of America

Library of Congress Cataloging in Publication Data

Yeadon, David.
Hidden corners of the Mid-Atlantic States.

Includes index.
1. Middle Atlantic states—Description and travel—
Guide-books. I. Title.
F106.Y4   917.4′04′4   76-30417
ISBN 0-308-10286-X
ISBN 0-308-10297-5 (pbk.)

10 9 8 7 6 5 4 3 2 1

North

0 10 20 30 40 50 100 150

THE COAST
1. Ocean Grove and Cape May
2. Mount Holly and Vicinity
3. The Pine Barrens
4. Greenwich and Vicinity
5. Mauricetown and Vicinity
6. New Castle
7. Odessa and Vicinity
8. Port Deposit
9. Chestertown and Vicinity
10. Cambridge and Vicinity
11. Smith Island
12. West Ocean City
13. Tangier Island
14. Northern Neck
15. Smithfield and Vicinity

THE MOUNTAINS
16. Blairstown and Vicinity
17. The Mercer Mile: Doylestown
18. Honesdale and Vicinity
19. An Outdoor Country Music Festival
20. Coudersport to New Milford
21. Hawk Mountain Sanctuary
22. Huntingdon to Lewisburg
23. Leesburg and Vicinity
24. A Flour Mill
25. Warm Springs and Vicinity
26. Abingdon and Vicinity
27. An Appalachian Coal Town
28. Danville and Vicinity

25

LYNCHBU
ROANOKE

27

DANVIL

26

KNOXVILLE

WINSTON-SALEM

CONTENTS

Virginia

Exploring Hidden Corners

Silence. It must unnerve some people. I spent most of the Bicentennial year roaming the back roads of five Mid-Atlantic states, and had expected to run into all kinds of problems with traffic congestion and busloads of tourists peering into every historical nook and cranny. I was very much mistaken. The well-known cities and coastal resorts were, true to form, disastrously jammed. Williamsburg was worse than Disneyland. Washington was one long waiting line. Philadelphia was a huge parking lot. But out in the countryside, only a few miles from the freeways, there was peace—total peace. No one was there. If I saw a motor coach it was racing as fast as it could for the nearest stretch of crowded beach. Families I met in some of my favorite villages, up in the hills away from the coast, were invariably "grabbing a bite" en route to some famous national showplace. They rarely paused to look around. They somehow managed to screen out the beauty. They resisted the stillness—kept the radio going, kept the kids busy and kept themselves in a state of constant expectation of some new experience down the road.

I wandered for thousands of miles among the mountains, along the seaplains, up in the Piedmont. I found another country, an America unknown to most travelers and understood only by those who live there or by those few individuals who take the time to explore it and talk with its residents.

The meaning of America and its heritage came alive to me in those months of travel. I saw history not in the dry, hackneyed terms of famous paper documents, proclamations, declarations and Washington-size figures. Rather I found it in local tales about local incidents and local people. A well-known American historian once wrote, "Look to the land, look to the people on the land. There is your history." Dr. Henry Mercer, whose magnificent museum at Doylestown, Pennsylvania, is mentioned in this book, began his vast collection of domestic, agricultural and crafts artifacts back in the 1890s. He wrote: "Here we have history presented from a new point of view . . . you may go down into Independence Hall in Philadelphia, and stand in the room in which the Declaration of Independence was signed. But do you think you are any nearer the essence of the matter there than you are here when you realize that ten thousand arms, seizing upon axes of this type made it worthwhile to have a Declaration of Independence by cutting down one of the greatest forests in the north temperate zone?"

The little explored countryside of the Mid-Atlantic states has a wealth of local history. It also contains some of the most beautiful landscape in America. If you can stand the silence, the slower pace of life out here; if you like pausing on a whim to chat with farmers or owners of old country stores; if you enjoy eating hearty country dinners at inns that most guidebook writers would never find—if you like all these things and more, you are a true hidden-corners explorer, and this book is written expressly for you.

Let's travel together through these five states, avoiding all crowded tourist centers, most "preserved" villages and over-publicized historical sites. Let's keep to the back roads wherever possible and go in search of the "real" America.

We'll visit little known coastal towns; we'll peep into old Quaker meeting houses, attend an outdoor country music festival, explore forgotten towns along Delaware Bay, talk with oystermen, investigate the mysterious Pine Barrens of New Jersey. We'll visit a community with all the charm of Williamsburg but none of the crowds; we'll wend our way along the winding streets of an old Susquehanna river town, explore the tiny Tidewater villages where "King" Carter reigned, take ferries out to the islands of the Chesapeake where the crab fishermen live, eat real Virginia country ham in Southside. Then we'll go up into the mountains and trace canal routes through steep valleys, tour an old lumber camp, find the remains of a settlement once built for Queen Marie Antoinette of France, visit a country town during its Bicentennial celebration, and meet the strange inhabitants of a hidden mountain valley. Up in the Virginia hunt country we'll find remnants of the Civil War era. We'll visit a flour mill still in operation, bathe in naturally hot springs in old spa towns, explore a "mountain empire," barter with fruit for a theater seat, walk up the blackened streets of an Appalachian coal town, and watch the bidding at a tobacco auction in the Bright-tobacco belt.

At times we'll pause to rest. We'll sit by quiet lakes, in fields overlooking mountain valleys or on the tops of rocky ridges, watching eagles spiraling on the air currents. Together we'll enjoy the stillness of the countryside. We'll meet familiar figures of American history in unusual places and guises. Better still, we'll meet unfamiliar figures whose impact on the nation's heritage was equally great.

We'll find an America unknown to most people. We'll have tales to tell, and we'll experience that special glow that comes from discovering places most guidebooks ignore.

It's fun—this hidden-corners exploration. May you enjoy all your journeys.

Travel Tips

Maps: Generally, the oil company maps of individual states are adequate for locating most of the places mentioned in the book. For real back roads travel, obtain more detailed maps from tourist information centers, or county maps from local government and highway department offices.

Road Signs: Signs often are rare on the back roads. There seems to be an assumption that the only people traveling in these areas are local residents who don't require such extravagances. So the hidden-corners explorer should rely on maps, common sense and a willingness to stop and ask questions. I found local people usually friendly and helpful. Of course, in some of the less inhabited stretches you may just have to put up with getting lost occasionally. I discovered some of my favorite places by throwing away the map and just roaming at will. It's a good way to get invited to dinner. No one can resist a poor lost traveler.

Accommodations: There are abundant reliable guidebooks providing information on restaurants, inns and hotels throughout the five-state area, although most are limited to facilities close to main routes and popular tourist centers. In the back country there's always an element of chance. You may find a glorious old inn serving splendid regional cooking and offering four-poster bed accommodation. Alternatively, you may have to make do with a campsite or a detour to the nearest highway town. Most of the hidden corners are in fact located within a reasonable driving distance of such places, so you should have no problems.

Historical Sites and Other Tourist Information: This book is not intended as a guide to tourist-oriented facilities. These are normally indicated on most travel maps of the five states, and guidebooks and pamphlets that describe such facilities are available in abundance at bookstores and tourist information offices.

The Coastal Region

1. OCEAN GROVE AND CAPE MAY
Contrasts on the Coast

Ever felt like a change from the overcrowded resorts on the New Jersey coast? If so, visit these two quiet and unusual seaside towns. Ocean Grove is located approximately eight miles south of Long Branch on Route 71, and Cape May is at the extreme tip of Cape May Peninsula, off the Garden State Parkway.

A sign on the dining room door, neatly hand-lettered, reads: "No Bare Feet And No Curlers." The fifty or so elderly individuals inside staunchly plowing their way through lunch would no more dine in bare feet or curlers than they would paint graffiti on the wall of the local Methodist church. The sign is really for the benefit of that rarest of creatures—a newcomer to Ocean Grove. "It is essential for the well-being of ourselves and our community that strangers learn our ways as quickly as possible." So I was informed by a tall gentleman with a large white moustache and tweed jacket—more like an English country squire than a tourist on the New Jersey coast. Victoria Davis, manager of a local inn, put it another way: "We're a strange little town. We like things to stay the way they've always been." So there are signs everywhere—little reminders of appropriate behavior: "Please Remove Your Hat When Entering The Hotel"; "Jackets Required For Din-

ner"; "Only Two Minors Allowed In The Store Unless Accompanied By An Adult" (a candy store); "No Disrobing On The Beach." Perhaps the most notorious requirement of this upright community is its weekend restriction on automobiles. From midnight Saturday to midnight Sunday no car is allowed on the streets. All must be either in private garages or driven outside the gates that guard the entrances to this small ocean community. Chains are pulled across, no traffic is allowed in and, according to local ordinances, no "work" may be undertaken by the residents for that sacred 24-hour period. There are specific restrictions, too, on lawn cutting, window washing, house painting, and car cleaning and even a ban on newspaper deliveries—although a court case of considerable magnitude is building over this particular issue.

Ocean Grove is indeed "a strange little town." It all began in 1869 when a group of 26 laymen and Methodist ministers incorporated the Ocean Grove Camp Meeting Association under special New Jersey State legislation and proceeded to develop the community as a permanent camp meeting ground and summer seaside resort. It was a reflection both of the popularity of large religious meetings during the late nineteenth century and of the growing reaction against other more notorious resorts that were beginning to line the New Jersey coast. The city of Long Branch, farther to the north, was a leader in seaside debauchery. From the 1830s until the end of the century the urban population of the Northeast poured in here seeking revelries of every kind—dancing, drinking, gambling, fast driving along the famous Blue Drive, faster women—even the attentions of the first professional gigolos in America. Huge resort hotels, rivaled only by those of Saratoga, were constructed along the oceanfront. Celebrities swarmed through the town in elaborate limousines. Diamond Jim Brady romanced Lillian Russell here; the Guggenheims and a score of other wealthy families built ornate mansions in extravagantly landscaped grounds; President Grant made the town the national summer capital. Other Presidents, including Hayes, Harrison and Wilson, loved the spirit of Long Branch and spent much time here.

But not the staunch Methodists. "Enough!" they said, and set out to create their own model community farther down the coast. Even today the character of Ocean Grove has changed very little. The large gates bear bronze plaques with the sonorous greeting: "Enter Unto His Gates With Thanksgiving And Into His Courts With Praise." Visitors immediately sense that this is no ordinary seaside town. There are no flashing neon signs, no Ferris wheels, no taverns, no hamburger stands, no clam bars, no amusements on the boardwalk. Instead one discovers cameos of an almost forgotten past: wide, tree-shaded streets, Eastlake and Gingerbread-style clapboard homes behind delicate picket fences, old Victorian hotels with wide terraces, clear vistas of beach and sea. The traffic moves slowly; elderly couples sit on benches in shaded parks; boarding houses are called The Quaker, The Sampler Inn and Fisherman's Cove (the biblical Fisherman, of course).

I remember the two elderly ladies crocheting on a porch, their chairs rocking in unison; guests at a boarding house enjoying a buffet lunch to the sound of hymns on a gramophone; the dignity and grace of the old homes facing Wesley Lake on the northern edge of the town; the total silence of Sundays and the amazing sight of carless streets.

The center of the community is the 7500-seat Great Auditorium, constructed in 1894 without the use of nails (in the tradition of Solomon's Temple). This magnificent structure contains one of the largest organs in the world and is surrounded by scores of tent cottages. These tiny structures, half tent and half wooden shack, are a reminder of the days when most of Ocean Grove was a real tent city, filled with canvas creations of all shapes and sizes. During the fervid summer weeks of worship these cottages can be rented from the Camp Meeting Association, and in the afternoons and evenings, between seemingly endless sequences of concerts, services, sermons and recitals, the occupants gather in groups under the shade trees between the "tents" to while away the time before the next event. Others sit on the benches lining the wide pathway that links the Great Auditorium with the beach.

Ocean Grove, once described as "God's square mile of health and happiness" is by no means to everyone's taste. Many consider its ordinances, particularly those that ban the use of the beach on Sundays, to be unnecessarily repressive. Others love it because of this very stability and feel themselves secure within its confines. Come and see for yourself. Whatever your feelings, you will be in for a most unusual experience on the New Jersey coast.

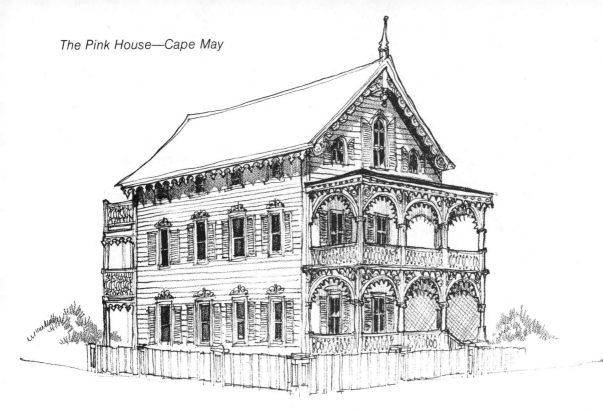

The Pink House—Cape May

The same things could be said of Cape May, although the spirit of this delightful resort tends to be a little more frivolous than that of its somewhat somber counterpart to the north.

The town is located at the tip of Cape May Peninsula, south of Wildwood. Way back in its early days the area was known as Cape May Island, but as it grew in popularity its name was abbreviated.

In many respects Cape May still retains a distinctly insular character. The town's architecture is almost totally Victorian; in fact it is one of the few classic examples of an authentic Victorian community remaining in the United States today. Stroll along the boardwalk, almost devoid of those crass commercial outlets so familiar in the northern resorts, and admire the magnificent old hotels generously endowed with towers, turrets, ornate balconies and terraces, carved Corinthian columns, elaborate shingle patterning, eaves dripping with delicate tracery and trellicework. The great Congress Hall, set back from Beach Avenue in its own large grounds, is one of Cape May's most durable hotels. It was first erected in 1812 and has survived many subsequent fires and enlargements while serving as a vacation "White House" for at least six Presidents. Today it's a quaintly outdated structure, always suffering from minor ailments but still one of the most popular places in town. Its high corridors and spacious rooms contain a strange mixture of elaborate antique furniture—great Baroque bureaus and richly wrought chandeliers—juxtaposed with nondescript couches covered in brilliant red vinyl and bowls brimming with plastic plants. There's a series of anterooms

Typical street scene—Cape May

off the main corridor: a television room, filled with late-nineteenth-century wicker furniture; a tiny card room, with velvet wallpaper and Tiffany-style lamps; and a small theater for recitals and concerts. On one occasion when I was at Congress Hall I noticed a handwritten sign on the bulletin board by the reception desk: "All plumbing will be turned off at 9:30 A.M. for repairs. Breakfast will be an hour earlier." One of the guests had scribbled, "Not again!" in red ink on the sign. Outside, workmen were trying to fix one of the tall columns supporting the mansard roof. It seems there was some danger of imminent collapse.

Yet the great old hotels continue to flourish, along with a dozen or more recent additions. A federal renewal grant has enabled the creation of an attractive mall in the old Victorian downtown area. The Historical Committee and County Art League have worked strenuously to preserve the finest examples of mid- and late-nineteenth-century architecture and have organized walking and trolley tours through the town. In addition there are do-it-yourself walking tour brochures that enable visitors to stroll at their own pace past more than 30 of the most magnificent Victorian buildings on the New Jersey coast—the exotic Chalfonte Hotel, the Victorian Mansion on Columbia Avenue, the unusual Emlen Physick House (normally open to the public) and, around Congress Hall, a superb collection of homes, including the ridiculously elaborate Pink House, now used as an antiques-and-gifts center.

There was a time when Cape May was merely one of a series of tiny "bathing places" on the coast. Hotels, restaurants and boardwalks were unknown in those days. Visitors slept overnight in "halls," according to this account from an old issue of *Lippincott's* magazine: "The customs of those earlier times were very primitive and democratic. Large excursion parties of gay girls and festive gentlemen would journey together and would upon arrival, bear down upon the ocean, ducking and splashing in old suits of clothes . . . the major-domo of the Atlantic Hall would send out to see what neighbor had a sheep to sell; the animal found, all the visitors of the male sex would take turn to help him dress [skin] it. Meanwhile parties of foragers would go out among the farmers around, ravaging the neighborhood for Indian corn. . . . At night, when dead-tired after the fiddling and contra dances, the barn-like hall was partitioned off into two sleeping rooms by a drapery of sheets. The maids slept tranquilly on one side of the curtains, the lads on the other."

In the mid-1800s steamboats began running regular excursions to Cape May from Philadelphia, and by 1866 the resort was linked to major East Coast cities by rail. Boom time had arrived. Flurries of hotels and boarding houses were erected. Fires were commonplace, but even the total destruction of the magnificent Mount Vernon Hotel in 1856 did not deter progress. The town kept on growing, attracting Presidents, celebrities and the whole hoi polloi of Victorian society. Local carpenters competed to produce the most "picturesque" architectural styles, which bore only fleeting resemblance to the more traditional vernaculars. They improvised to excess, using the most exotic forms of carpenter Gothic derived from the popular "pattern books." To their clients, particularly the nouveau riche whose summer residences clustered along the confusing network of streets behind Beach Avenue, architectural extravagance was an appropriate expression of wealth and status.

And yet, ironically, when it came to excesses in behavior the same individuals were irrefutably modest. The codes governing bathing were particularly strict. Segregation of the sexes was obligatory. When the white flag was flying, ladies could bathe in suitable attire. This often consisted of more than seven yards of material—enough for a fair-size tent. The "nine-piece" bathing suit was considered the minimum in propriety. Some ladies never even emerged from their bathing wagons, which were drawn into the sea so that they could dip their feet in the water through the open floor. When the red flag was raised, ladies were expected to leave the beach exclusively to the gentlemen, who pranced together through the waves in coverall costumes.

Gradually, as other more contemporary resorts developed in the 1900s along the New Jersey coast, Cape May experienced a period of decline. It was regarded by many as "hopelessly Victorian," and had it not been for the enthusiasm and imagination of local citizens and council the town might have quietly slumbered into permanent eclipse. Fortunately it didn't happen. Homes and hotels were beautifully restored, the mall was created, the boardwalk improved. Today it's once again a flourishing community with a totally unique appeal. This will never be a Wildwood, an Ocean City or an Atlantic City. It exists for those who enjoy the fun of the beach coupled with the refined charm of a Victorian village. May it, like Ocean Grove, never change.

2. MOUNT HOLLY AND VICINITY
History Just off the Turnpike

Here's an unspoiled area of New Jersey, full of history and almost within the Philadelphia-Camden conurbation. It is located directly across the Delaware River from Philadelphia and is bounded on the north by Trenton and the New Jersey Turnpike, on the south by Route 70, on the east by the Fort Dix Military Reservation and on the west by the Delaware. Towns within the area include Mount Holly, Burlington, Bordentown, Columbus and Crosswicks.

It was a Thursday morning, very hot and sticky. My cat, Boots, who accompanies me on most of my journeys, was decidedly unhappy with the weather. He tried lying under the camper in the shadows, then hiding under the seat, then stretching full length across the table by the open window. Finally he chose the lower shelf of the refrigerator. I went off to explore the Columbus Farmers Market, leaving him between a honeydew melon and a bag of New Jersey tomatoes, with one foot extended holding the refrigerator door ajar.

The market is a major event in the western portion of Burlington County. It's located just outside the village of Columbus, about 10 miles north of Mount Holly, and is open every week Thursday to Sunday, with an especially large flea market on Thursday. And what an event this is! Outside, in an arc around the enclosed

Helis Stock Farm—near Jobstown

market area, a hundred stalls, fold-down tables and car trunks provide instant display space for old teapots, Art Deco mirrors, records in faded glossy sleeves, partial sets of encyclopedias, cut-price household cleaning products, home-made jewelry, back issues of *National Geographic* magazine and mounds of chipped, cracked, buckled, dented and overpriced "antiques." The bellowing, bawling, pushing, nudging crowd moves like molasses between the displays. The ice cream stall does a rapid trade. Exhausted bodies lie prostrate in its shadow surrounded by Coke bottles and discarded wrappers.

". . . Hey, stop shoving back there! . . ."

". . . Yessir, that camera works like new. See this photo? I took it with that camera only last week. . . . No lens? Well, it's what's known as interchangeable. . . . Here, this should fit. . . . Just get a pair of pliers and . . ."

". . . One fer a dollar, two fer a dollar fifty, three . . ."

". . . You buyin' or not, sir? You're keepin' other people away . . ."

". . . This machine slices, chops, dices in seconds . . ."

". . . Just take a look at these bikinis. . . . Hey, a special deal for you, look at the label, from Paris, yeah, three bucks. . . . Look, I'll throw in a jar of sun lotion. . . . Hey, come back! . . ."

". . . Not twenty dollars, not ten, not five, not even three dollars, here we go, for this genuine cut-glass decanter set, the bargain of a lifetime . . ."

". . . Herb, for God's sake, give 'er an ice cream . . ."

". . . Next time? There won't be no next time! This is crazy . . ."

It's only 8:30 A.M., and there's a crowd at Kate and Al's pizza parlor waiting for thick, runny slices of pie. Many of the customers are drinking beer. At the Italian Bake Stand three large men in white aprons, sweat tumbling in torrents off the ends of their noses and chins, stuff breads and pastries of unusual shapes and dimensions into brown bags—Dutch cheese squares, French pretzels, bagels, popovers, babkas, challah, apple turnovers.

Inside the market is even more crowded. The homemade-pickle shop is just opening up, and nibbling samples are being laid out on top of the barrels. Across at Mullen's Seafood Stand two pretty girls are preparing the day's cauldron of clam chowder. Steam and the aroma of fresh-chopped herbs waft over the countertop. An older man arranges platters of deviled crabs and porgies in the parsley-sprinkled display cabinet. Farther down, a stall bulges with boxes, crates and sacks of every conceivable kind of vegetable and fruit; piles of green-striped watermelons tower over artfully arranged trays of plums, nectarines and bananas. The air is thick with the smell of roasting chickens, newly brewed coffee, pizzas, beer and cheap cigars. And the day has hardly begun!

A few miles to the east at the world-famous Helis Stock Farm, near Jobstown, the day is half over. Horse trainers like to run their charges in the early morning when the air is cooler. Manager Clarence Grimes believes in the time-honored methods of horse rearing: "To get a champion, breed the best to the best and hope for the best." Pierre Lorillard, the tobacco magnate who founded the race-horse estate in 1872, spent a number of fortunes perfecting breeding techniques. To Lorillard money was merely a means to an end ("No gentleman can live on less than one thousand dollars a day"), and when his colt Iroquois won the 1881 English Derby he lost interest in his Rancocas Farm and pursued other "ends." He returned later to reestablish his estate, which he oversaw until his death in 1901.

Then Harry Sinclair took over this "Camelot of the Thoroughbreds," demolished the extravagant Lorillard Mansion and, after a brief jail session following his involvement in the Teapot Dome Scandal, returned to see his prize horse Zev, win $270,000 in one season. The estate was sold in 1943 to the "Golden Greek," an oil wildcatter named William G. Helis, and today it continues to be run by his family. Visitors are welcome but are asked to register at the office before exploring the stock farm. Strangers to the area should have no problem in spotting the entrance—it's a magnificent Baroque gate, said to have come from the original Bowery Bank in New York City.

Bordentown

By far the most memorable building is the half-mile indoor racing track, which also serves as a foaling shed. It's an amazing piece of design and craftsmanship, one of the largest wooden structures in the eastern states and somehow indicative of the enthusiastically lavish way in which America's entrepreneurs pursued their pastimes. The whole estate smacks of restrained opulence. Its 90 miles of fencing, its finely detailed barns, even the little Victorian Gothic office building, all reflect an era of confident and calm prosperity.

Yet, in contrast, the history of this part of Burlington County is characterized by tumult, revolt and dissension. The Revolution in particular left its dinstinct imprint on the region. It divided towns, friends and families. Most notable in the last category were the Franklins. William Franklin, Benjamin's son, was at that time royal governor of New Jersey and was greatly distressed by his father's anti-Tory stance. Protesting "alarming transactions and rebellion" in the region, he refused to remain in the capital, Burlington, and retired to his residence at Perth Amboy until he was formally deposed on June 25, 1776. Burlington, Bordentown and Mount Holly all saw action against the British and Hessian armies. Bordentown suffered through occupation by Scottish troops, when space was at such a premium that ten or more soldiers were often billeted in a single tiny cottage. Cannonballs flew with random regularity. The meeting house on the green at Crosswicks boasts one of them stuck in its northern wall. Burlington was bombarded by its own gunboats to drive out Von Donop's Hessian troops, and Mount Holly, a sedate country town today, was the scene of the ferocious Iron Works Hill Battle on December 23 and 24, 1776. Although the battle was officially a victory for the Hessians, Von Donop soon realized that he and his 2000 men had been decoyed by a small troop of Americans, while a few miles to the north Washington was invading Trenton in a gloriously successful maneuver that resulted in 1000 Hessian prisoners and the capture of six cannon and "a thousand stands of enemy arms." There were other skirmishes in this area throughout the war, but few matched the Mount Holly battle for courage and tactics.

The Revolution by no means ended the region's apparent attraction for dissenters of all political and philosophical hues. Quakers had first arrived here in significant numbers from England in 1677, following a brief visit by George Fox in 1672, who described the area as "a most brave country." Persecution had at the time reached fever pitch in Britain, and even some of the New England colonies had little patience with the strange and silent ways of the Friends; in 1659 four were hanged on Boston Common for "participating in most strange and blasphemous rites." William Penn's conversion in 1666 led to the establishment of safe refuges in the "middle colonies," and by the 1690s West New Jersey was a stronghold of the religion. John Woolman, born near Mount Holly, later became one of their most noted spokesmen. His *Journal* is still a popular book today, and his "walking journeys" on behalf of slaves helped solidify opinion against "this peculiar institution." The famed "Underground Railroad," an elaborate system of secret routes and hideouts that enabled slaves to escape from the South to the North, flourished in the area. Some of the homes around Crosswicks, for example, still possess hidden rooms where slaves were kept until they could be transported to the next safe house on their journey north.

Equally as anxious as the Quakers for a place of refuge was Joseph Bonaparte, brother of Napoleon and formerly King of Naples and Spain. He arrived in America on August 28, 1815, following the calamitous French defeat at the Battle of Waterloo. He settled on a knoll by the river near Bordentown and lavished his fortune of jewels, gold and paintings on the creation of an elaborate mansion and grounds. He even had a sumptuous boat built for his regular river excursions. But somehow he never quite gave up the concept of Napoleonic destiny. Although he himself seemed to have little taste for power (he refused a serious offer to become King of Mexico), Joseph spent much of his time championing the cause of Napoleon's son before dying in Florence in 1844. All that remains today of his opulent enclave is the small Bonaparte Park Garden House in Bordentown.

One of the more interesting contemporary rebels in this "hotbed" region is a gentleman named Mahalchik, who resides in a large wigwam on the edge of an armed forces dumping ground near Columbus. He has devoted much of his time to creating an "anti-establishment" display of placards, paintings and protests against current political conditions in America. He uses elaborately constructed three-dimensional tableaus, complete with dressed-up tailor's dummies, old cannon and even a couple of steam locomotives, to illustrate key elements of his protest, although recent vandalism and lack of maintenance have diminished their impact. His own newspaper, *The Freedom Fighter,* is normally available for sale when Mahalchik is at home. Many dismiss him as a madman. Local officials ignore him, but travelers invariably stop to wonder at the energy and forthrightness of the man.

Quaker meeting house—Mount Laurel

Pond scene—Collier's Mills

But let's forget the revolts and the dissensions which seem to have characterized the region's history and, instead, journey slowly along its quiet country lanes and visit some of its attractive towns and villages. For this area, though so close to the "urban corridor" of the East Coast, has changed little since the eighteenth century. Burlington, Bordentown and Mount Holly, for all their contemporary prosperity, have managed to retain that air of spacious sedateness and calm that characterized regional market towns during the horse-and-buggy era. Farnsworth Avenue in Bordentown is a perfect period piece combining, in one harmonious whole, architecture of the Colonial, Georgian, Federal and Victorian eras. The Historic Society has prepared a short walking-tour pamphlet that describes 25 historic homes and sites in the town. Besides the Bonaparte Park Garden House, one of the most popular places of pilgrimage is the Thomas Paine House, at the corner of Church Street and Farnsworth Avenue. It is said that the opening line of Paine's *The American Crisis*—"These are the times that try men's souls!"— became the battle cry of Washington's soldiers at the Battle of Trenton.

These walking tours are a popular feature of towns in the region. Mount Holly is particularly well endowed with historic structures, including its delightful courthouse (1796), designed by Samuel Lewis (architect of Philadelphia's Congress Hall); its County Prison (1810)—now a museum—and the John Woolman Memorial (1783). One of my favorite buildings, though, is away from the historic zone. It's the richly detailed Frederick Kelly Mansion, at Bispham and Charles Streets. Not many visitors come here, but the house has unforgettable charm, if Victorian architecture is to your liking.

The long slope of High Street from Mount Park to its junction with Garden Street is

one of the most distinguished segments of urban design in the region. It contains, as does Farnsworth Avenue in Bordentown, a remarkable array of mansions, yet the width of the street coupled with the almost unbroken canopy of shade trees provide unifying elements that allow architectural variety to flourish with spatial consistency. Truly a masterpiece.

Away from the larger towns are a number of attractive villages where the dominant element in each case is the old Quaker meeting house. The one at Mount Laurel was erected in two segments, the older part in 1760. The interior is typical of meeting houses in the region—unpainted walls, unpolished wood paneling and pews, tall, unadorned columns supporting a stark gallery and, most notable of all, an ingenious system of vertically operated screens and doors to permit the division of the space into two equal but separate halves. There is no decoration, no color, no unnecessary detailing. Yet in its spartan character the house evinces purity, honesty and simplicity—values the Quakers revered.

The meeting house at Crosswicks, situated on a beautiful open green, and the one on High Street in Mount Holly are almost identical internally, whereas the one in Rancocas, a charming village to the west of Mount Holly, is smaller and even more simple in design.

Villages of exquisite beauty can be found whichever way you travel. Imlaystown, Smithville, Vincentown, Columbus—all are perfect examples of small, unspoiled agricultural communities. Lakes and ponds abound. One of my favorite is at Collier's Mills, east of New Egypt—but just follow the tracks or handpainted signs and you'll find your own. I'm constantly amazed that this lovely area can exist so close to the freeways and just across the river from Philadelphia.

A track in the Barrens

3. THE PINE BARRENS
The Elusive "Piney" People

New Jersey's Pine Barrens are a strange tract of sand, pine trees, streams and swamps occupying the central section of southern New Jersey. To the north is the Fort Dix Military Reservation, to the east the New Jersey coast, to the south Route 30, and Philadelphia lies a short 25 miles to the west. Communities within the area include Atsion, Indian Mills, Chatsworth and the restored iron-producing village of Batsto.

There is no silence quite like the silence of the Barrens. On a hot day when the wind dies, the pines stand motionless; ferns droop; ponds and lily-topped swamps lie still without ripples. Nothing moves in the wasteland. Sandy paths gleam bright white in patches and meander into the gloom of the forest. Even the flies—monstrous in size and appearance—retreat into the fissured bark of the pine trees. The aroma of resin hangs heavy. A snake sleeps in a comfortable coil shaded by a rock.

To the casual motorist or coast-bound tourist, the Pine Barrens of New Jersey are a rather dull interlude along a highway normally littered with billboards, gas stations, and fun-food restaurants. The interminably straight pavement, lined with dwarf pine and oak, rises only occasionally to present vistas across the Barrens—and then only of more pines and oaks. Accelerators are pressed to the floor and children, anxious to reach the sea, are told to be patient.

But those who take the time to wander the Barrens find a region bursting with history, legend and strange tales of even stranger people who live deep in the recesses of the forest. There was once a Robin Hood of the Pines who plagued the region, stealing from the wealthy landowners and giving to the poor. Regrettably, Joe Mulliner's brief career was terminated at the end of a rope after he kidnapped a wealthy heiress and demanded a ransom of whole-hearted affection from the confused lady. She was returned safely a day after her capture but it was never altogether clear just how the ransom had been honored. Joe didn't have time to explain, and the lady, in true ladylike fashion, declined to discuss the incident.

Then there's the story of the "Jersey Devil," a cloven-hoofed enigma whose antics seem to be as varied as the individuals who claim to have seen it. A composite picture of the creature, which seems to spend most of its time in the Barrens region, includes features of a bat, kangaroo, horse and serpent. Some claim it has a distinct appetite for human flesh, while others endow it with the gentle characteristics of an elderly philosopher whose favorite occupation is the discussion of ethics and politics with learned men of the state.

Tales abound of pirates, smuggling ventures up the Mullica River deep into the Pines and, during Prohibition, illicit stills down sandy tracks visited by mobsters in long black Cadillacs. But perhaps most curious of all are the tales about the Pineys themselves—the hermitlike inhabitants of the Barrens, who have attracted disproportionate attention.

"The Pineys? I'd use that word careful in these parts if I was you." So I was warned by a bartender in a rundown roadside tavern near Batsto. "Folks don't take too kindly to being called Pineys by outsiders. Too many wrong things bin said about 'em. Too many clever 'fessors snoopin' 'round these woods. Should mind their own damn business, I say."

It's true. "Pineys" is a much maligned word for a much maligned people who, over the generations, have developed a lifestyle of self-dependence in the forest. Attention was first directed to the region in 1913 with the publication of Elizabeth Kite's paper on the inhabitants of the Pine Barrens, in which she presented a psychological profile of resident families. Their ancestors, she suggested, may have been early colonialists who abandoned the coastal plantations to seek greater personal freedom in the back country. Later they were joined by Tory renegades, deserters from the British army during the Revolution and members of notorious "banditti" gangs who plagued the area during the 1800s. Other outcasts, criminals and adventurers from the cities on the fringe of the Barrens gave the forest dwellers a reputation for licentiousness, indulgence and illegal activities. Marriage was virtually unknown; inbreeding led to an unusual degree of feeble-mindedness and mongoloid characteristics among the young, and hunters brought back tales of abandoned revelries deep in the forest.

Ms. Kite's carefully documented study was grotesquely sensationalized. Reporters and pseudoscientists flocked to the Barrens to view this alien culture firsthand and vied with each other to produce the most startling accounts of primitive degeneracy. The Pineys meanwhile retreated deeper into the forest and became more and more suspicious of outsiders. They continued their frugal existence, making charcoal and gathering sphagnum moss, cranberries and swamp huckleberries for sale to local markets.

It was only following the construction of paved highways through the Barrens and the establishment of the Fort Dix Military Reservation to the north that the Pineys began to be assimilated into contemporary society; but even today, deep down the narrow back roads, there are those who prefer the silence of the forest to the jingle-jangle world outside. They don't particularly welcome visitors and have a distinct aversion to snoopers, and any stranger using the expression "Piney" might just end up with a backside full of buckshot! Best to leave them in peace.

More rewarding is a visit to the restored village of Batsto on the Mullica River. Here the history of the Pines comes alive. During its heyday, from the mid-1700s to the mid-1800s, the Pines possessed an abundance of thriving communities situated along the Mullica and its tributaries, all frantically involved in the smelting of iron from locally mined "bog ore." A wide range of goods were produced, from cannon balls for the Revolution to stoves, kettles, tombstones and farm

implements during more peaceable times. Batsto, one of the larger communities in the area, was founded in 1766 by Charles Read of Burlington, a wealthy speculator who recognized the potentials of bog ore. He constructed a furnace and designed long, shallow-draft barges known as shallops to haul the ore from the nearby swamps along the narrow creeks for smelting. The furnace changed hands a number of times; during the early years of the Revolution it was owned by an ardent patriot, Colonel John Cox of Philadelphia, who supervised the casting of munitions for the Revolutionary army. The British never managed to quench the furnace fires of Batsto, and during one abortive expedition in 1778 they had to make do with destroying the village of Chestnut Neck, way over at the eastern outlet of the Mullica River near Smithville. This only served to emphasize the strategic position of the furnace; the men employed there were even exempted from military service so that production levels could be maintained.

Gradually during the early 1800s the Pittsburgh region became the nucleus of iron and steel production, and smaller centers such as those in the Pine Barrens developed other industries, including the production of glass and paper. A large factory at nearby Atsion was also used variously for cotton processing and cranberry sorting. But by the 1860s most enterprises had failed, furnaces had fallen in, villages were abandoned or burned and the forest closed in over the cellar holes. Nearby, at Indian Mills, is the first Indian reservation in America, established for the Leni Lenape Indians in 1758, which once boasted a population of more than 700. Today Atsion has 16 permanent residents—although the restoration of part of the original settlement, and the campsite along the adjoining lake shore, bring life back into the area for a few brief summer weeks. Batsto could have been lost like a score of other communities, but when the state acquired a large portion of the Pine Barrens in the 1950s, an ambitious restoration program was initiated. Today visitors can tour the elaborate ironmaster's mansion and stroll down the hill past a score of other exhibits to the rows of sturdy workers' cottages west of the lake. It's a fascinating and authentic restoration, and those interested in New Jersey history will find an abundant selection of publications in the visitors' center. The restored bog-iron village of Allaire, a few miles to the north near Asbury Park, should also be visited.

To the east, at Smithville, is a more commercialized but equally attractive "living museum" assembled around the 1787 Smithville Inn. It presents, in 30 old structures specially moved to this site, a picture of eighteenth-century village life and crafts. The nearby Smithville Theater, housed in a vast striped tent, offers a varied selection of top-name shows throughout the summer for the delight of coastal tourists.

Although most of the manufacturing industries have long since left the Barrens there is still considerable activity in the blueberry fields and cranberry bogs deep in the forest. "Old Peg-Leg John" Webb, a local schoolteacher, was the first to cultivate cranberries here in 1845 in a former swamp he had drained for use as a meadow. By the 1870s the fine art of cranberry cultivation reached an economic peak. Another rash of communities spread over the Barrens, with such strange names as Ong's Hat, Double Trouble and My Misery. Joseph White published his *Cranberry Culture* in 1885; it immediately became the accepted au-

Ironmaster's mansion—Batsto

thority on the subject. His daughter, Elizabeth, promoted another industry in the Barrens by cultivating blueberries.

Today cranberries and blueberries grow side by side throughout the area—one of the highest-yield regions in the United States. And yet the Barrens are still largely underdeveloped. Cultivation occupies a tiny fraction of the 650,000 acres of this strange wilderness. Within minutes of leaving the main highways one can be lost in the forest. It's very easy to forget all sense of direction and time on those twisting soft-sand tracks often leading nowhere or, more perplexing still, to a maze of forks and sidetracks that penetrate ever more deeply into the gloom.

Yet the area has a gentle beauty all its own. Ponds and lakes abound, their brown "cedar waters" lapping lily-rimmed banks. From the tops of occasional rises or, better still, from fire towers, vistas stretch in all directions of endless miles of unbroken forest. The ground itself, carpeted by pine needles, is as soft as cushions, the air fresh and full of the scents of the forest, like the bouquet of a full-bodied wine—which leads to a final recommendation for a side journey. To the south at Egg Harbor City is the Renault Winery, one of the oldest American wineries, in continuous operation since 1864. An informative tour is offered and a full description given of the still-wine- and champagne-making processes. Then, as a highlight, the tasting room is opened for the benefit of visitors. Even if you're not a lover of the Lambrusco variety of grape nor particularly anxious to sample such concoctions as Blueberry Duck, Noah Blanc and Pink Lady, the winery itself is well worth the visit and is an excellent way to round off a journey through the New Jersey Barrens.

4· GREENWICH AND VICINITY
A New Jersey Tea Party

Boston was not the only town to hold a tea party. Come and explore Greenwich, center of the small region located between the Cohansey River, south of Bridgeton, New Jersey, and the eastern shore of Delaware Bay near Salem. Route 49 is its northern boundary. Communities within the area include Greenwich, Bayside, Roadstown and Hancocks Bridge.

This could well be a corner of England. The Cohansey River wends its way through Constable country—flat meadows edged with groups of perfectly shaped elms rich in foliage and full of shade. Summer clouds billow high above the salt marshes. Through the trees a church steeple rises up from a cluster of old wooden buildings. A picket fence, sparkling white in the sunshine, defines a small cottage garden set about with box trees and hollyhocks. One almost expects the hay wain to come lumbering along the lane, and the comfortable mooing of cows on their way to the milking shed. Tennyson could have written sonnets here; Wordsworth would have found his muse.

Greenwich itself, set close against the river, typifies the unspoiled character of the region. Founded in 1675 by the Quaker John Fenwick, the community developed in linear fashion along Ye Greate Street, and its fine collection of homes

Cohansey River near Greenwich

has changed little since the 1700s. Many are marked with plaques indicating the name of the original owner and the date of construction. The magnificent Gibbon House, built in 1730 for Nicholas Gibbon, a maritime merchant from London, is an excellent example of the early Georgian style. In common with a number of other estate homes and farmhouses in the area, Flemish bond brickwork was used throughout with an interesting pattern of alternating pink and blue headers and stretchers. Today the house is headquarters for the Cumberland County Historical Society and has been attractively arranged as a museum of late-eighteenth- and early-nineteenth-century domestic artifacts (open to the public Monday through Friday 9 to 4, Saturday and Sunday 2 to 5).

Across from the Gibbon House is a classically simple 1852 structure, originally built as a Presbyterian meeting house and now used occasionally as a lecture hall by the Historical Society, and farther along on the opposite side of the street is the old stone tavern, erected in 1728. This is one of a number of stone structures in the village. The Philip Dennis House (1765), the Dr. Levi Bond House (1725) and the little stone school on the northern edge of the community are all examples of confident craftsmanship by stonemasons. Farther to the east near the town of Cedarville is the region's largest stone structure, a Presbyterian church erected in 1780. The dark brown color of the stone suggests a high iron content—it is possible that it came from a quarry on the edge of the Pine Barrens close to a source of bog ore (see "The Pine Barrens").

Gibbon House—Greenwich

One of the finest homes in Greenwich is the Ewing House (1834), situated near the old marketplace in the center of the village. For complete contrast, there's a reconstructed Swedish granary (*c.* 1650) on the grounds of the museum. These two buildings alone tell much about the area's history and pace of economic development. The Swedes purchased a vast tract of land between Cape May and Swedesboro (east of Wilmington, Delaware) from the Indians in 1640. Scattered trading posts were developed along the Delaware River, but the enterprise was poorly managed and many settlers lived in appalling conditions, sometimes even in muddy caves along the banks of the river.

The structure on the museum grounds was brought, log by log, from a farm at Dutch Neck, four miles from the village. Carl Lindborg, a fine-arts professor and authority on Swedish settlements in early America, helped in the reconstruction and claims that the granary is the only one of its kind still existing in the country.

Much of the early Swedish culture was destroyed by Dutch colonizers who dominated the area from 1665 until the English takeover in 1674. However, mailboxes in the small villages along the Delaware still reveal a distinct Swedish heritage in the region. Ed Dubois, manager of the nearby Bait-Box Restaurant at Hancocks Harbor, claims that until recently families of Swedish-descended "river gypsies" were a familiar sight along the bay creeks. They lived in shallow-draft "shad skiffs" or "sharpies" and made a living from itinerant fishing and oyster "drudgin'." He went on to describe the period during the early 1700s when the Cohansey and adjoining rivers were favorite sheltering areas for coastal pirates.

The names of Black Beard and Captain Kidd occur again and again in local folktales. Caskets of stolen treasure are said to lie buried beyond the river marshes in the firm ground of the upland meadows. Black Beard's booty should be an interesting find. Legend has it that wherever he hid one of his treasures, the notorious pirate always buried two men along with it to guard it. His ghost (or at least the ghost of a similar counterpart) is still said to hover around the site of his winter quarters at Back Neck; and the Pirate House (1734) in Greenwich is said to be haunted by a pirate who was murdered here by partners he had double-crossed.

This sedate community slumbering in the shade of great maples and elms has indeed a more turbulent history than one first might imagine. It is particularly renowned for its contribution to the rebellious spirit of the colonies prior to the Revolution. The date was December 12, 1774. A British brig, the *Greyhound,* quietly sailed into the port of Greenwich and unloaded tea at the house of a Tory, Dan Bowen. The Boston Tea Party of the previous year had received wide attention, and captains were anxious to unload their troublesome cargo as unobtrusively as possible. Greenwich was selected as a quiet, peaceful place well removed from the centers of dissent. But unfortunately the captain had underestimated the local populace. Forty young men of the town disguised themselves in "tea-party" fashion as Indians, raided Bowen's House, removed the tea and held a ceremonial burning in an adjoining field on December 22. Thus was the flame of revolution kindled, and the names of the tea burners are immortalized on the monument in the market square.

Unfortunately, other Revolutionary exploits in the area ended more disastrously. Particularly notorious are the events of March 20, 1778, at Hancocks Bridge, about 15 miles to the west of Greenwich. Following a skirmish at nearby Quinton Bridge when the British were driven into retreat by the Cumberland County militia, the British commander, Major John Simcoe, made a surprise attack on the Hancock House and massacred without mercy most of the rebels sleeping there. William Hancock, a Tory and owner of the house, was also mistakenly killed by the British. Today the house, preserved as a museum, is a grim reminder of one of the Revolution's more unpleasant incidents.

To explore the twisting country lanes of the Cohansey region, first take the narrow road across the flat marshes to Bayside. Although today this is merely a rather unusual collection of beach shacks and old piers, imagine the scene a few brief decades ago when it was the town of Caviar, center of America's sturgeon fishing and caviar industry. At the height of its prosperity almost 6 million pounds of sturgeon were caught annually, and over 100,000 pounds of caviar were sold in the eastern cities or exported to Europe.

Joe Hancock, a descendent of Samuel Bacon, one of the original settlers along the Cohansey in 1682, related to me the demise of the industry: "We did what we always do—we gave it away. Russians came over to learn how to make proper caviar. We taught them everything we knew, then off they goes, back home, and they don't need us no more. They got cheap labor and plenty of their own sturgeon. We do the same thing all the time." Joe, who describes himself as "old and bitchy," has a wealth of information on the area. He owns the Bait-Box Restaurant at Hancocks Harbor and, when he's around, loves to show visitors his old photos of Bayside as it once was (these are now placed around the walls of the restaurant). Until a few years ago he even featured sturgeon steaks on his menu. "Old Jack Wheaton usta fish 'em for me. He was the last one to go after sturgeon. Shame no one does it now. They're back in the bay again, y'know. Once in a while they'll drag one up—makes a hell of a mess of those light nets." Judging by the old photos of "small" six-foot sturgeon and the sturgeon "hides" that Joe proudly displays on a shed by the restaurant, it's a creature that demands respect and a lot of know-how to catch. The Bait-Box Restaurant is well worth a visit for a dinner of broiled fresh weakie (sea trout) or croaker or bluefish, or whatever the local fishermen have caught that day.

Or maybe you'd prefer a swim? If so there are a few beautiful bathing ponds in the area, most of which are known only to the locals. Near Jericho on the way to Quinton is a lovely roadside lake, but my favorite is down a sandy path just outside Shephards Mill. There's no sign, except for an occasional handwritten notice of bathing hours, and you can't see the pond from the road, so drive slowly.

As you leave this delightful region pause briefly in the old-fashioned community of Roadstown near Route 49 and look out for the Ware House. Here in the late 1700s Maskell Ware began the manufacture of his famous chairs from swamp maple and local marsh rushes. These cane-bottom ladder-back chairs came to represent all that was best in American rural industry—strength, dependability and dignity. Subsequent generations of Wares continued their manufacture into the late nineteenth century with only minor modifications. "Uncle William" Ware, for example, made " a dainty chair" from thinner vertical posts, whereas Dan Ware used different types of wood, including cherry and chestnut. Unfortunately there's no Ware family museum in the village, but occasional exhibitions are arranged by the local historical society. Meanwhile life continues its steady pace in this quiet corner of Cumberland County.

Bayside

5. MAURICETOWN AND VICINITY

Ode to the Oystermen

Here's a forgotten corner in southern New Jersey, once the center of Delaware Bay's oystering industry. It lies along the Maurice River south of Millville and Vineland and is bounded on the north by Routes 47 and 49 and on the south by Delaware Bay. Communities in the area include Mauricetown, Bivalve, Dennisville and Fortescue.

King Nummy, last chief of the Unalachtigo Indians, would hardly recognize his kingdom today. The coastal portion along Delaware Bay, from Green Creek southward to Cape May, is rapidly developing as a sequence of ticky-tacky towns filled with beach homes, gas stations, crab stands and New York-style deli stores. Of course in 1700 when he sold his land to the settlers and moved to his own private island on the Atlantic side of the peninsula, King Nummy was in no position to predict some of the more unfortunate outcomes of national progress and prosperity.

To the north and above Dias Creek, the more commercial characteristics of the lower peninsula give way to a landscape of low, flat marshlands and gently undulating meadows, dotted with clumps of trees. Here we find delicate Victorian-flavored villages such as Dennisville and Mauricetown; an old nineteenth-century lighthouse, currently being restored as a maritime museum; a few tiny communities of shacks huddled along the seashore on the far side of the marshes; a couple of forgotten seaside resorts, and, along the Maurice River, the sad remnants of the once flourishing oyster industry. It's a fascinating area, worthy of study and slow exploration.

Let's start with Mauricetown itself, once the hub of the region and home of sea captains and boatbuilders. The finest mansions are lined along the river bluff, and most have been restored by their occupants. The Compton House, built in the early 1800s, has a fine mansard roof and exceptionally ornate elevational trimmings. Many of the neighboring homes fall within the "carpenter Gothic" category, and some possess elaborate wrought-iron detailing—an unusual feature of the town. High Street has a number of antique stores. The headquarters of the Maurice River Historical Society is located in the Mauricetown Academy (1860), just up the street from the post office. Occasional exhibitions are held here but to date the community doesn't seem particularly anxious to attract tourists. Residents claim they have enough problems with the trucks that pour through the town carrying the spoils of a nearby sand-and-gravel operation. So, with the exception of specially organized tours, none of the homes are open to the public on a regular basis. Nevertheless the town is worth a visit—and there are lovely short walks to be enjoyed along its tree-lined streets.

The oyster industry that once brought prosperity to the river is currently operating

Mauricetown

Bivalve

at a severely reduced capacity because a parasite, known as MSX, wreaked havoc upon oysters in the offshore planting beds. I chatted with one of the oystermen who still frequent the Bivalve wharves. He was a gentleman of the old school, full of stories of the oyster schooner races that used to mark the beginning of the busy spring "planting" season. The oystermen would be up around three in the morning and out of "Long Reach" (Bivalve) by dawn, anchoring beyond the harbor before tucking into sturdy breakfasts of pork chops, eggs, thick slices of red Virginia ham, fried potatoes, boiled mackerel and coffee. Then they would race up the coast to the official seeding grounds and work at a frantic pace until sundown, "drudgin' " the small seed oysters for deposit in the planting grounds to the south. As the oysterman told me, "Why, them boats, there was m'be four, five hundred of 'em, they was so thick you could walk from one side of t'river to t'other, steppin' from one boat to t'next. And could those gen'l'men handle 'em—every boat slot right in place, not a scratch, not a tickle. An' there wus only a few inches between 'em. Yessir, they really knew boats in them days."

Once the spring planting is over the oysterman can do what he pleases until the fall, when once again the fleet sets out on its predawn voyages, this time to the planting grounds for the oyster harvest. In the early days the fleet consisted of a motley collection of shallow-draft boats, all designed along the same lines as Indian canoes: shallops, sloops, dredgeboats, skipjacks, bugeyes. During the 1870s, however, the river area was linked to Philadelphia by rail and the demand for fresh oysters increased dramatically. In the early 1900s more than 90 carloads of oysters a week were run to Philadelphia from Bivalve. The miscellany of

smaller "drudgin' " boats gave way to specially designed schooners. In 1905, 588 of these vessels were recorded in the Maurice River—the largest concentration of schooners in the world. Today there are fewer than 40 power schooners on the river, and only a few of these actually work the beds.

The adjoining communities of Bivalve and Shell Pile tell a sad story. At Bivalve most of the shucking and iceing plants down by the river are silent. A couple of clamming establishments remain open, and the owners don't mind visitors coming to watch the shelling, chopping and packing process. But there's little sign of oysters except for huge volcano-shaped piles of gleaming white shells rising up above the swamp grass. Shell Pile is appropriately named—many of the poor clapboard shacks are resting on foundations of crushed shells. They are inhabited mostly by blacks living in dire poverty. I talked with an elderly man in the Belle Monte "restaurant," a lopsided green shanty with a long black chimney ("Any Kind Of Food Any Time Of Day"): "Lawd knows things can't get much worse 'round here. Take a look at Port Norris." (I did. That once prosperous town above Bivalve is a very sad remnant of former glory.) "No damn oysters, so no damn work and so no damn nothin'. That's what it feels like around this part of the river country—"nothin'." Nothing happens. There's the occasional brawl down at the breeze-block bar by the end of Bivalve Road. Offenders end up on a "flag list" pinned to the wall. The worst penalty is to be barred entrance. "Hell, then nothin' gets to be real nothin'!"

Of course, there are optimists. Employees at the local Fish, Game and Shell-

Fisheries Office on the Bivalve wharf still keep signing a full quota of annual fishing permits—and, as lessors of the 30,000-acre offshore oyster planting grounds, they have recently increased the annual fee to $1.50 an acre. So, someone must be catching something somewhere.

About 15 miles to the east of Mauricetown is the sedate village of Dennisville, once a major shipbuilding center along this stretch of coast. Large schooners with three "stickers" (masts), up to 1000 tons in weight, once littered the tiny, marshbound Dennis Creek. Apparently its proximity to sound shipbuilding timber and away from turbulent sea breakers made it an excellent location for boat construction.

Adjoining the creek in the surrounding swamplands Dennisville's second major nineteenth-century industry flourished. Four or five feet below the surface were the preserved remains of a giant white-cedar forest. Hand-split shingles made from cedar logs dug out of the swamp with such unusual implements as "progues," "butters," "mauls" and "froes" were popular for their durability. The roof of Philadelphia's Independence Hall was once re-covered with 25,000 of them, and the wood occasionally was of such high quality that it was used in the manufacture of violins.

Today Dennisville is a designated historic area and contains an interesting collection of eighteenth- and nineteenth-century homes along its dignified, tree-lined main street. To the south, the community of South Dennis has a distinct New England flavor. One of its homes was supposedly constructed from bricks carried as ballast by a British merchant ship that visited the area before 1812.

Over to the west, beyond the Maurice River, are two almost forgotten seaside resorts, Fortescue and Sea Breeze. Both have seen better days, but the Hotel Charlesworth at Fortescue continues to serve fresh seafood and homemade cakes—although some of the more traditional dishes of the area, such as soup made from the blood-red meat of snapping turtles, muskrat potpie and weakfish (sea trout) roe, are no longer featured on the menu. However, I had the chance to try out one of these dishes. Al Dowe in the nearby bay community of Villas rented me one of his cottages for a few days. On one occasion he returned from a fishing trip in his unique "float boat" dragging eight huge "weakies" behind him. "Just missed a manta ray, she was a good two hundred pounds." According to Al, the bay is teeming with mantas, sharks, sturgeon and whales, not to mention the ubiquitous jellyfish and horseshoe crabs that are washed up on the beach by the thousand every high tide. After cleaning his catch he presented me with a ready-to-fry three-pound weakie, complete with two pieces of pink roe, which I immedi-ately prepared in a simple butter-lemon sauce. Glorious! Everyone who has the chance should try these delicacies.

One of my favorite haunts in the Maurice River area is the lighthouse at East Point. With the exception of two unusual little beach communities, Moores Beach and Thompsons Beach, views from the restored cupola are of mile after mile of flat green marshland. Patches of the tall grass surround the marsh meadows where salt hay is cut during the summer. Herons stand upright in the reeds, wait-ing for lunch; turtles waddle across sandy paths and plop into swampy ponds.

The lighthouse was built in 1846 as a guide for oystering boats, but after World War II it fell into disrepair and in 1972 a combination of vandalism, fires and Hur-ricane Agnes all but demolished the building. The Maurice River Historical Soci-ety then decided to restore it for use as a maritime museum. I chatted with Ev Tur-ner, coordinator for the project. "It's been a heck of a struggle, but so far we've raised over ten thousand dollars and rebuilt most of it, based on some old plans we found. Everyone's been marvelous—local companies have all chipped in. Ev-erything was done at cost. There's going to be a lovely museum here." It's a bit of a detour out to the Point, but well worth the extra few miles if only to gain a van-tage over the bay marshlands and enjoy the unusual character of this New Jersey corner.

East Point Lighthouse—near Delmont

6. NEW CASTLE

New Castle, Delaware, is located on Route 9 approximately seven miles due south of Wilmington.

For all the long and important history and the remarkable beauty of this small town, New Castle is still relatively undiscovered. Visit and explore before the bus tours come.

There's an excellent "Heritage Trail" guide available at the courthouse that provides a brief history of the town and a sequential description of the important buildings. Omitted from the guide, though, is one of my favorite structures, the octagonal library just opposite Immanuel Church.

Surprisingly, this quiet community with its lovely bayside park, its flower-filled gardens hidden behind white fences, its quiet cobblestone alleys and brick sidewalks, possesses a turbulent past. It's a past that reflects in microcosm the lively story of early colonial America. Originally established as a fort by Peter Stuyvesant in his fight against local Swedish colonists in 1651, the settlement then briefly reverted to the Swedes and a year later, following a second skirmish, emerged as a Dutch town with the name of New Amstel. The British captured it in 1664 and renamed it New Castle. The Anglo-Dutch war of 1673 led again to a brief change in ownership, but the following year it was back in British hands and in 1682 was William Penn's place of disembarkation. Although Penn brought with him charters from Charles II and the Duke of York deeding him Pennsylvania and "the three lower counties on the Delaware," the Delawarians demanded and gained home rule in 1704, and New Castle became the seat of government. A period of prosperity and peace ensued until the Revolution, when British troops came too close to the town for the comfort of the politicians, who promptly transferred the state capital to Dover. Nevertheless New Castle continued to grow. The War of 1812 had little impact. The great fire of 1824 was followed by the creation of a larger town, and in 1832 it became a railroad terminus. It was not until later in the nineteenth century, when Wilmington began to emerge as the dominant Delaware city, that New Castle entered a twilight phase. New construction was minimal after that time. The town was comfortably cocooned for almost a hundred years until the recent restoration was initiated.

Various scenes—New Castle

7. ODESSA AND VICINITY
The Quiet Delaware Coast

Next time you venture into the Delmarva Peninsula, avoid Route 13 and take the lesser known roads along the eastern coast, particularly around Dover, New Castle, Odessa, Delaware City and Woodland Beach. Here's an area full of history, folktale and residents with long memories.

"Nobody much comes down this way now." I was talking with a retired oysterman at Leipsic. "I remember the way it used to be, though. Family had a sturgeon business, they was great fish—some more 'an three hunnert pounds. They sent that caviar stuff up to Philadelphia for treatin'. Couldn't stand it m'self; still, there's no accountin' for taste. Now muskrats. Tha's somethin' else. No one catches 'em anymore now, but there was a time, not so far back, when these marshes—" (he waved his arm across the reeds, ponds and creeks stretching away to a misty horizon) "—when they was covered with muskrat sheds. Seems nobody likes 'em much anymore."

Local residents will also point out the old country mansions, once surrounded by acres of peach trees. They'll talk of the great duck shoots, the 20-pound snapping turtles, the huge hauls of shad at Port Penn and other nearby marsh villages, the steamers and sidewinders from Philadelphia and of the "Big Thursday" cele-

brations that opened the oyster season in August at Bowers Beach.

Today much of the life and activity of past years has gone. The fishing industry is in decline, and oysters are plagued by a mysterious ailment (see "Mauricetown and Vicinity"). Resort activities have moved farther south to the Rehoboth Beach–Ocean City coast; serious sturgeon fishing disappeared decades ago, and many of the proud country mansions have long since crumbled into the reeds. Yet the area retains a distinct charm. While it lacks the conscious sophistication of the western Tidewater peninsulas, there's a peace here, a gentle rhythm of life; there's character in the rough, tacky shacks and wharves of the marsh villages, dignity along the quiet streets of Odessa, Delaware City and New Castle.

We'll begin our journey up this forgotten stretch of coast at South Bowers, just south of Dover. Here a quiet community of cottages on stilts overlooks the more active harbor across the river at Bowers Beach. This was once an important oystering center, but now it seems to be better known as a saltwater anglers' resort. Strangely enough, there's no bridge linking the two villages across the narrow creek.

"Oh, we could have one if we wanted," I was told by a South Bowers resident. "They keep askin' us, the authorities, y'know, but we don't want any of those bars and restaurants like what the Beach has got. It's just fine the way it is now." So to cross the few feet from South Bowers to Bowers Beach means a 14-mile drive through the marshes and cornfields of Kent County. Fortunately there is at least one interesting feature en route, the Island Field Archeological Museum, where a partially excavated Indian cemetery has been enclosed for public viewing (weekdays April through October, 12 to 5). In addition to well-documented displays of artifacts there's a brief slide show that describes the lifestyle of these primitive marsh dwellers. Although relatively unsophisticated compared with midwestern tribes of the same period (A.D. 500–1000), these "Webb-Phase" people amassed a large collection of implements and artifacts as a result of extensive trading links with groups in New England, New York State and even as far away as the Mississippi Valley. There is also evidence, in the way the cemetery is laid out, of a clearly defined social hierarchy. The more important members of the group were given deep burials and accompanied by a large number of grave offerings. Children also apparently had similarly high status, while the women of the tribe seem to have been treated with far less regard. Few objects have been found in their shallow graves.

The Webb-Phase people seem to have vanished from the area around A.D. 1000, and it was not until several hundred years later that vestiges of the Leni Lenape ("Original People") settled here, oblivious of the marshlands' previous residents. These were the Indians that early Swedish and Dutch settlers encountered on the Delmarva Peninsula and in southern New Jersey. Their fragile civilization was inevitably destroyed by the land-hungry colonists. Disease wiped out large numbers, and the remainder moved westward or accepted sanctuary in the reservation at Indian Mills (see "The Pine Barrens"). A few intermarried with blacks and "po' whites" on the peninsula, creating unusual groups such as the "Moors" who collected in the "Down Sockum" area near Millsboro. Pride in their heritage was such that until recently those claiming to be of Indian descent demanded their own schools. In 1922 they established the Nanticoke Indian Association to preserve the traditions and practices of their Indian ancestry.

Bowers Beach is just one of a series of tiny coastal villages separated from the mainland by stretches of open marsh. Cries of egrets echo over the wastelands. Few cars travel the winding, potholed roads. Herons rise languidly from reed-enclosed pools and circle, barely moving their wings. Those strange prehistoric creatures, horseshoe crabs, with long, spiked tails, glide across the muddy bottoms of saltwater creeks. A breeze as fresh and clear as the cloudless sky sets the reeds rattling. A duck glides over the ripples, followed by ten youngsters in a line. Turtles bob their stony heads above the water to watch the passing scene.

Much of the marsh area is protected from indiscriminate hunting by reserves at Woodland Beach, Bombay Hook and Little Creek. Viewing towers provide vantage points over the flat, treeless wetlands. Occasional hummocks, tiny islands of higher ground covered with dense vegetation, punctuate the endless plains. When the wind blows, the reeds rise and fall in unison, like waves on some great green ocean.

Straggled out along the beach like shipwrecks are scores of cottages, some built from scraps of lumber and metal sheeting, others ingenious expansions of old trailers. At Kitts Hummock there seems to be a mosquito problem. Elaborate

Shack with birdhouse—Kitts Hummock

houses for the mosquitos' prime enemy, the martin, have been constructed in the windblown gardens behind the dunes. It's a lost place, where people seem to come for no particular reason and just stay. I chatted with a year-round resident outside his trailer shack. He was middle-aged, almost toothless and very thin. He was sitting in a cracked and tape-bound rocker surrounded by beer cans and old newspapers. "Jes' can't seem to get away. I've got too much to do 'round here." I couldn't see any sign of activity. "Gotta put another room on before winter." He pointed to the only part of the old trailer that was still recognizable. "Gonna knock a door through there." He paused and took a long gulp at his can. "Jes' wish they'd bring that damn'd lumber. They's so damn'd slow—and I ain't fetchin' it!" He lay back in his chair and picked up a scrap of newspaper almost a month old. "No, I'm damn'd if I'm fetchin' it."

There's not much left of Port Mahon, farther up the coast. According to the locals, it used to be a popular place in the early years of the century. The large wooden building on iron stilts was once a lighthouse and, before the area became a small oil unloading depot, there was a beer garden there. Today it's a haunt of fishermen, who launch their boats at a ramp farther along the channel through the reeds. In contrast, Woodland Beach, to the north, has retained much of its charm as a small village, complete with green and pond. Like most other places in the vicinity, it's usually very quiet—an ideal spot to drowse away a warm afternoon.

The marsh villages seem all but forgotten, but adjoining Route 9 are three notable historic buildings that do attract the occasional tourist. The John Dickinson

Mansion, close to the junction with the Kitts Hummock road, is set among carefully laid-out gardens and is an excellent example of a plantation house, with a Georgian flavor. Dickinson, the "Penman of the Revolution," President of Delaware (1781–1782) and later Chief Executive of Pennsylvania, spent much of his youth here, and later restored the house after a severe fire in 1804. A few miles up the road is a very rare example of a stone-built octagonal schoolhouse, with a central chimney and a small shuttered window in each wall.

The Allee House, down an unpaved road off Route 9, is preserved by the state as an example of the vernacular architecture of eighteenth-century Delaware. It is said to have been built in 1753 by Abraham Allee, son of a Huguenot refugee from Artois, France. Like the Dickinson Mansion, it is a reminder of the days when Delaware was an area popular with descendents of European gentry, when their mansions dominated the flat coastal landscape and slaves worked the peach orchards of their wealthy estates.

To appreciate the flavor of those days, one should explore the old river port of Odessa on the banks of Appoquinimink Creek. Although the community is rather more "discovered" than the area to the south, the majority of travelers still roar along Route 13 oblivious to its presence. But what a lovely place this is!

Main Street slopes downhill from the noisy road and traffic lights to the river curling its way through a small, reed-filled valley. The street is spacious, lined with broad shade trees behind which lie an array of homes in various architec-

tural styles. Most impressive are the Corbit-Sharp and Wilson-Warner homes, both late-eighteenth-century Georgian Colonial structures. I spent a delightful hour being escorted around the former by a diminutive lady with very bright eyes and a genuine enthusiasm for the artifacts displayed in the house, particularly the tall clocks crafted by Duncan Beard, a local eighteenth-century clockmaker and silversmith. She spoke of him as if he were still alive. "This is one of his favorite pieces—look at the beautiful workmanship. He's still not appreciated enough. It must be awfully upsetting for him"—she paused and colored a little—"Well, I'm sure he knows."

Unfortunately most of the homes remain closed to the public except for special open-house occasions such as the popular "Christmas in Odessa," usually held in the first week of December. Nevertheless, just strolling the streets you can sense the spirit of the old port: imagine river wharves lined with schooners and steamers, parties at the hotel on Main Street to celebrate successful business deals, the squeaking and crunching of carriages carrying gentlemen to and from the dockside offices. Vast agricultural fairs attracted thousands from New Jersey and Maryland. Local land values soared and the town boomed—boomed until the late 1800s, when the emergence of the steam engine put an end to river commerce. The residents fought against the railroad and, in doing so, lost the opportunity to gain a terminus. Odessa, like so many other river towns, was prematurely fossilized. Today we benefit from the abrupt termination of progress in enjoying an almost perfect example of an eighteenth-century community.

Octagonal schoolhouse—near Dover

A similar fate overtook Delaware City to the north. When the Chesapeake and Delaware Canal opened amid lavish celebrations in 1829, the town had readied itself to become the new Philadelphia. Unfortunately the almost simultaneous completion of a competitive railroad system limited local growth. Nevertheless the ambitious little community continued to expand its industries—shipbuilding, peach warehousing and distribution, sturgeon and shad fishing, the construction of Fort Du Pont across the canal. Then in 1919 the federal government purchased the canal and set about widening and deepening it. In doing so, officials decided to move its entrance two miles to the south of Delaware City and thereby destroyed all dreams for a great bay metropolis. The old stretch of canal is now used as a small marina, and in the center of the park by the ocean is a huge cast-iron "diving bell" used for repairing the old lock gates. Tourists still come, but mainly to catch the ferry across to Fort Delaware on Pea Patch Island out in the bay (Wednesday through Sunday, April 14 through October 17). Construction of this vast granite pentagon was begun in 1848. It was used most actively during the Civil War, when adjoining barracks housed more than 12,000 prisoners.

Delaware City is typical of this coastal region—a town full of history and peace, a community almost forgotten. Just the kind of place hidden-corners explorers love.

The kitchen, Corbit-Sharp House—Odessa

Architectural details—Port Deposit

8. PORT DEPOSIT

Port Deposit, Maryland, on the Susquehanna River, is located about 3 miles north of Route 95 and 30 miles northeast of Baltimore.

Here's a splendid remnant of an old river town. It began modestly as a ferry point and mining town. Then as the northern hinterland was stripped of its timber, Port Deposit became a major lumbering center. Canals and railroads consolidated its prosperity, and by the mid-1800s it boasted a population of more than 2000. Locally mined granite was used to build numerous churches in Philadelphia and Baltimore. Herring and shad were caught in enormous nets in the river.

Jacob Tome, Port Deposit's number-one prominent citizen and benefactor, was an excellent example of the American success story. He arrived in town in 1833 on a raft. Without capital or education he created the largest lumber business in the area and then went on to become one of the leading financiers of the state. The town is full of his buildings—great granite edifices crammed along the narrow strip of land between the river and the mountainside. His foremost contribution was the Jacob Tome School for Boys, whose ornate copper tower peers over the trees on the hillside above the town.

Take time to stroll through this unusual community, with its terraced gardens, its embellished steps linking Main Street with High Street, its old mill, the Tome schools and churches. Visit the Port Shop, in an elaborate eighteenth-century mansion; fish from Ray Spengler's dock; watch barge building in progress, or sit and count the cars as the trains thunder and howl their way past the docks.

Port Deposit has seen better days, but there are few river towns on the East Coast that can match its sturdy Victorian character and the drama of its setting.

Street scene—Chestertown

9. CHESTERTOWN AND VICINITY

Wandering Through Kent County

Kent County, Maryland, is a peninsula (although some refer to it as an island) at the northern extremity of the Delmarva Peninsula, just north of the Chesapeake Bay Bridge. Chestertown is the county seat. Other communities include Rock Hall, Fairlee, Betterton and Galena. Allow plenty of time to explore Chestertown—its a place you won't forget.

Chestertown, home of the famous Washington College, is all that a Tidewater town should be. Approached by the long, low-arched bridge across the Chester River, its brick-and-white-wood mansions stand proudly on the shore bluff. A church steeple rises above spreading elms, and boats roll gently in the water. An elderly lady holding a poodle on her lap suns herself on a verandah in a large wicker chair while a maid in apron and cap sweeps the steps leading down to a perfectly mown lawn.

This could be Savannah or some other equally refined southern town. It certainly has all the relaxed dignity and architectural harmony of a Williamsburg. Take a stroll down its tree-shaded streets—so shaded that along some of the narrower ones the sun rarely pierces the thick canopy of branches and leaves. Note the unusual brick sidewalks. Thick moss and tiny grass shoots grow up between the cracks in the meticulously laid herringbone patterns. Big brass doorknobs, freshly polished, reflect every detail of the street; brick-and-stone steps lead up to the heavy oak doors of a Georgian house constructed in the Flemish bond manner, with just a trace of ivy to relieve the austerity of the architecture. Farther down, a more feminine mansion, with Victorian trellicework and a richly carved Italianate cupola, stands between two large maples. A privet hedge and white paling fence assure the front garden of privacy from the street, while manicured box trees march in line to the steps leading up to the porch.

There's a do-it-yourself walking tour that all interested visitors should take. Many of the finest homes and other buildings of historic interest can be found in the area bounded by Cross Street, High Street, Water Street and Maple Avenue. Most, though, are closed to the public except on special occasions such as the infrequent "candlelight tours." As might be assumed, the splendid merchants' mansions are located along Water Street, on the bluff above the Chester River. Widehall, at 101 Water Street, is a perfect example on the street side of the restrained Georgian style. In contrast, the rear of the house, facing the river, boasts a superb Ionic portico. Its first owner, Thomas Smythe, was head of Maryland's provisional government during the 1774–1776 Revolutionary period, and a subsequent owner, Robert Wright, was governor of Maryland from 1806 through 1809. Farther down at 107 Water Street is the large River House, a dignified mansion seemingly designed more as a Philadelphia or Boston townhouse, and one that would even do justice to some of London's exclusive Georgian enclaves. In this setting its urbanity looks rather misplaced, although the colonnaded

verandahs at the rear give it an entirely different appearance from the river.

Queen Street possesses some interesting eighteenth-century homes, in particular the Federal-style Nicholson-Deringer House and a Queen Anne-influenced dwelling at 105. Opposite, up narrow Church Alley, is a larger Queen Anne house, currently headquarters of the Historical Society of Kent County. This was once the home of William Geddes, from whose boat crates of tea were ejected during Chesterfield's own tea party in 1774. At the northern end of Church Alley is "Lawyers' Row," lined with the tiny, one-story wooden structures typical of so many county seats in the Tidewater region. A few lawyer's shingles do hang over the sidewalk—although most of the offices seem to contain real estate agents. At the end of the row, the junction of Court Street and High Street, is the blatantly Victorian Stam's Hall (1886). Most published town guides disdainfully ignore this prominent brick intrusion. I think it's delightful!

Chestertown's streets, the unencumbered dignity of its residences, its delightful High Street scenes, reflect an era when society possessed a confidence in its own values, a belief in its way of life, certainty in its future. Of course there were discrepancies. The poor were largely ignored—as to some extent they are today, if the dismal dwellings at the western end of Queen Street are any indication. In the eighteenth and nineteenth centuries poverty was accepted as an essential ingredient of the free enterprise system and created little guilt on the part of wealthier citizens. Today we claim to be more enlightened. Possibly—but our

modern towns and cities hardly reflect a new unity of purpose and ideals. For all the rhetoric, poverty is still very much with us.

Somehow, though, poverty in this rural area doesn't look so pronounced as in city slums. In fact, along the back roads of Kent County poverty takes on a somewhat picturesque appearance, and most legally poor residents would perhaps not recognize the expression—or the sentiment. People still live independent lives out here. Even though the peninsula is close to the East Coast urban corridor, it seems little affected by the twentieth century. The fishermen down at Rock Hall bring in their catches of crabs, oysters and softshell clams using some of the same methods and equipment as their grandfathers. The tiny resort of Betterton on the Sassafras River seems little changed since the days when steamers brought trippers there on day excursions from Baltimore. The large old hotel still broods upon the bluff, and steamed crabs and crab soup are served at the Crab Shack to today's trippers. Nearby at Turner's Creek Park an old granary stands down by the river, and not far away Knock's Folly has been restored as an interesting example of an early eighteenth-century country house.

It's a crisp, clean landscape. Cornfields stretch in regimented rows over the undulating fields. Unpolluted water laps the ochre-colored banks of the Sassafras.

Over in the village of Gratitude, near Rock Hall, Mrs. Williams serves family-style dinners in her home to a limited but discerning clientele. There's no sign. Visitors

have to search for the house, and advance reservations are normally essential. On the harbor at Rock Hall, restaurants provide the freshest of fresh seafood. The Chesapeake Restaurant is known for miles around for its huge and "correctly prepared" crabcakes. Along High Street in Chestertown, Bob Coleman's and Frank Kelly's delightful store, Flyway, specializes in hand-carved and -painted decoys (or "wildlife counterfeits," as they have been labeled by two of the most famous carvers, Lem and Steve Ward of nearby Crisfield). There are two wildfowl refuges in Kent County, both of them part of the national Flyway System of reserves that stretches from the Canadian border to the Gulf Coast. In October the Eastern Neck Refuge at the tip of Kent County and the adjoining Remington Farms Wildlife Management Area are filled with thousands of migrating ducks, geese and other birds from the north. Most popular is the beautiful black-necked Canada goose. Other species include mallards, pintails, snow geese, widgeons and teals. There's a do-it-yourself checklist available at the Eastern Neck information stand that lists all the birds recorded in the area and their periods of seasonal abundance.

When I took a July stroll across to one of the tree-covered hummocks in the Eastern Neck Refuge, I had to fight a running battle with hordes of biting flies. I, of course, came off worst but I'm expected to take these chances for the sake of the book!

A couple of beers and a crabcake down at the Rock Hall Harbor Restaurant soon restored my enthusiasm for the area and the project, so I moved southward to the next hidden corner.

Betterton

10. CAMBRIDGE AND VICINITY
The Crab Story

Ferries, country stores, old churches, crab pounds and tiny harbors–they're all here in this delightful corner of Maryland on the eastern side of Chesapeake Bay. Cambridge is located approximately 30 miles south of the Chesapeake Bay Bridge. The region encompasses the western portions of Talbot and Dorchester Counties and such towns as Easton, St. Michaels, Oxford, Hoopersville, Wingate and East New Market.

I shall always remember the Cambridge Jail. There it stands above the river, an imposing granite edifice with a castle-like tower and thick, barred windows—all that a jail should be: a physical expression of society's moral stability, a threatening presence to would-be malefactors. It appears, however, that the original architects, doubtless carried away with the powerful sturdiness of their creation, forgot one minor detail—the cells themselves face directly onto the street, and some are even located at street level. As a result the authorities have had to erect the sign: "No Talking To Prisoners From The Sidewalk." The sign doesn't seem to make much difference, though. When I was there three friends were carrying on an obviously hilarious conversation with an inmate, whose laughter poured in a chortling stream from behind the thick iron bars. Somehow the great stone edifice didn't seem so threatening after all.

Cambridge, the seat of Dorchester County, is a pleasant town. The business district is dull, at least architecturally, but there are some splendid nineteenth-century homes along Commerce Street, High Street and Mill Street. Marinas and boatyards occupy much of the river frontage. The road near the courthouse and the diminutive Lawyers Row are surfaced with brick, meticulously laid.

The sedate character of Cambridge reflects the region's long history. A few miles to the west of the town, for example, on Route 16, is the restored Trinity Church (c. 1675), one of the oldest Protestant churches still in active use in the United States. It's hidden down at the end of a cornfield by the river, so watch out for the signs. Also to the west, on Route 343, is a superb re-creation of a Post windmill. Resembling a two-story house supported by a single central post, such mills were a familiar sight in the countryside during the late eighteenth century.

The northern section of the Tidewater region was settled a few years after John Smith's exploration of Chesapeake Bay in 1608. Most of the early immigrants were English, and there's a touch of England even today in both the scenery and the towns. Talbot County, for example, which lies across the Choptank River from Cambridge, has long been one of the most traditional of the Tidewater counties. Long elm-lined drives lead to the elaborately colonnaded entrances of huge plantation-type mansions, and at the rear closely cropped lawns slope down to the waters of shallow inlets. The county is full of such inlets; they must provide satisfying seclusion for the wealthy home owners.

Lighthouse maritime museum—St. Michaels

The towns—Oxford, St. Michaels, Easton—all retain a charm and harmony of appearance that reflect the social stability and heritage of the area. Easton is located just off tourist-crowded Route 50, and St. Michaels, with its splendid maritime museum complex, is rapidly becoming a favored spot on the itinerary of travelers passing along the peninsula. Justifiably so—there's a splendid do-it-yourself walking tour here through the picturesque streets and lanes of the town.

Oxford, which can be reached directly from Route 50 or by taking the ferry from Bellevue on the St. Michaels Peninsula, was settled in 1669. It has been known variously as Williamstadt and Thread Haven. During the eighteenth century the port rivaled Annapolis as the busiest in the province. Many of the major London and Liverpool merchants established early trading branches here as export centers for the tobacco grown in the hinterland. Tobacco was such a stable economic item that it often replaced money as a basis for transactions. For example, the "T'read 'Aven" ferry was initiated in 1683 by a Richard Royston, who received 2500 pounds of tobacco for his services. Even in those days inflation was a significant factor: in 1685, according to county records, Isaac Sassarson was awarded double the amount, to "attend with a boate in Oxford three times a day for the bringing passengers of." In 1750, when the ferry was operated by a woman, Elizabeth Skinner, the stipend was 6500 pounds.

Take the ferry (cash, not tobacco, is required). The St. Michaels portion of Talbot County contains some lovely drives, particularly down the fingerlike peninsulas leading to such villages as Tilghman, Fairbank and Neavitt. The last is a center for clamming. Strange "mano" boats, with long pieces of pneumatic equipment suspended over their sides, are docked in a huddle around the short pier. Over at nearby Bellevue is a similar concentration of "trot-lining" boats for crabbing. Dockside conversations between the watermen are full of mysterious words and expressions. Some of the men have a tendency to call each other "honey," but that, I was informed, is a local linguistic idiosyncracy.

My initiation into the fascinating world of the watermen came when I was exploring Hooper Island to the south of Cambridge, in Dorchester County. This is an attractive part of the region, and one I will describe in more detail later. But first I want to tell you about crabs. I paused at one point to pick up some soda at Esther Dean's store, just north of Hoopersville. While I sketched the old-fashioned interior, the elderly lady behind the counter gave me an amazing monologue on the crabbing industry of Chesapeake Bay. Her information was later supplemented by other watermen, and I present the following account for those who, like me, try to understand what is going on around them. I should also point out that other hidden corners, including Smith and Tangier Islands, are important crabbing communities—so some basic knowledge of methods and terminology will help visitors appreciate these places a little more fully.

Chesapeake Bay is one of the crabbing centers of America, indeed of the world. According to government statistics the bay as a whole contributes more than half the national catch of blue crabs. Actual "whole weight" figures amount to some 70 million pounds, or approximately 200 million crabs. This of course is in addition to the huge hauls of oysters and softshell clams—particularly important for Maryland watermen, as their official crabbing season is limited to the period April 1 through December 31. The Virginians have no closed season, but winter crabbing methods are very different from the crab-potting techniques normally used in shallow water during warm weather. At the onset of the cold months the crabs scurry into the deeper portions of the bay and enter a period of semi-hibernation in the soft seabed mud. The only way to extract them is with Virginia's specially equipped dredging fleet.

Potting and dredging are only two of many ways to catch crabs. Other methods have been developed to reflect the changing antics of crabs during the different seasons and under the varied ecological conditions in the bay. Around Smith Island many of the older watermen enjoy Jimmy crabbing. A large male, or Jimmy, crab with a string tied around one of its legs is allowed to roam the shallows in search of female "sooks" (fully mature females that have shed their last shell). As the Jimmy finds a likely mate and grabs her, he is dragged back to shore by the delighted waterman, who promptly removes the lady friend and sends him back for another. Needless to say, his ardor soon diminishes—the waterman usually finds he needs a generous supply of Jimmies to gather a worthwhile catch.

Around Talbot and Dorchester Counties trot lining is a more popular process. Salted eel bait is attached at regular intervals along a thick line, which is then

Esther Dean's store—near Hoopersville

submerged. Crabs, attracted to the gristly meat, firmly grip the bait while eating, and when the trot line is hauled up they are lifted out of the water by hand nets.

Finally there's the scraping process, normally used during the spring when crabs have moved into the eel grass found in shallower water along the bay. A scraping device attached to the boat moves along the seabed and literally rolls crabs, eelgrass and anything else lurking in the murkiness into a carpetlike bundle, which is lifted out of the water for sorting.

Crabbing is a fascinating world unto itself. It has its own phraseology. Crabbers refer to the "first rush" (spring); to "reading" (understanding) crabs, and to crabs that "hang up" (die), usually when shedding. Crabs themselves are given all kinds of names, depending on their sex and maturity—there are number ones, Jimmies, she-crabs, snots, sooks, whales, slabs, punks, peelers, shedders, lemon bellies, ballies and busted sooks. Then of course there are the boats— skipjacks, bugeyes, dinkies, jenkins' creekers, bar cats, mano boats and hooper- island draketails.

To learn about the bay and its people, talk to the watermen and explore some of the lesser known peninsulas. For example, travel through the southern portion of Dorchester County, an important crabbing, oystering and clamming area un- known to most travelers. It's another world along the Honga River. Areas of marshland and "fast land" (firm ground) merge into one another. Groups of trees or, occasionally, large stretches of woodland denote the higher ground, but mostly it's long, open vistas across tall, waving grass. Communities are scat- tered. Many homes and small holdings are set back from the road along narrow paths. At times the marsh seems to encroach as far as their front doors. Near Hoopersville I noticed a couple of abandoned shacks that were slowly sinking into the soft mud at the edge of a brackish swamp. One particularly dilapidated dwelling bore the sign "Hooper Hilton"!

Here, families still retain graveyards on their own land. Where homes have been abandoned, headstones are left as mute reminders of past occupancy. Most are submerged under the weeds. One I came across had remained upright, stained by the elements. It read:

ANN TYLER
SO BELOVED
1807

It's more active down by the wharves, particularly during spring crabbing. Trot lining and potting are the most popular methods here, and there's some scraping for "peelers" in the shallow eelgrass coves adjoining the bay. Beautifully shaped skipjack boats rest against the piers waiting for the winter season, when its time for "tonging" oysters. Packing plants at Hoopersville and Wingate, on the op- posite side of the Honga River, turn out hundreds of round tins of crabmeat. The lids have a "window" so that buyers can check the meat for quality. Backfin is considered the best, but I've found the meat from "lemon bellies" (females full of eggs) to be equally delicious. On the wharves are pounds where shedders and peelers are kept and constantly sorted under running water until they climb out of their oppressively small hard shells and emerge as "softs"—the gourmet's delight.

The roads across the marshes are characterized by narrow wooden bridges that clatter alarmingly even when one obeys the 15-miles-per-hour speed restriction. The one linking upper Hooper Island to middle Hooper Island seems unusually fragile—although some of the others on the route north through the Blackwater National Wildlife Refuge are also distinctly shaky.

The refuge, like its counterparts in Kent County to the north (see "Chestertown and Vicinity"), is part of a chain of resting places for ducks and geese following the annual fall flyway from Canada. During late November as many as 100,000 geese concentrate here, and at least the same number of ducks. Some 30,000 normally stay for the winter; the remainder continue south in those famous V-formations to seek warmer weather and adequate food supply. For the photographer and nature lover Blackwater is an autumn paradise. Of course this is also hunting country. A sign at a gas station on the northern edge of the refuge reads: "Deer Checking Station Here."

Family plots on the "fast land"

There are two other points of interest in the area worth mentioning. Nearby Bucktown was the home of Harriett Tubman, a black slave who later became known as "the Moses of her People" for her role in the Underground Railroad. At the age of twenty-five she helped members of her own family escape, then subsequently made at least 19 other "transports," leading more than 400 slaves to freedom. Irate plantation owners put a price of $40,000 on her head, but she was never caught and went on to serve as a Union nurse and spy during the Civil War. There's not much to see in Bucktown except the historical marker, but the story of Harriett Tubman will live forever.

Finally, when leaving the region try to pass through the delightful village of East New Market, located east of Cambridge. There's an interesting range of eighteenth- and nineteenth-century architecture, including the 1790 Friendship Hall and the brick Manning House on Main Street, formerly a tavern and hotel. Again, like the larger communities, the town possesses a refined character, reflective of the region's long heritage.

11. SMITH ISLAND
Home of the "Softs"

Here's a real island in the middle of Chesapeake Bay, more than an hour's sail from the mainland. Come here to explore, to rest or to eat one of the largest lunches of your life. A ferry runs daily to the island from Crisfield, Maryland, on the Delmarva Peninsula, normally leaving at 12:30 P.M. and returning at 5:00. It is best to make reservations in advance during the summer (301-425-2771). Overnight accommodations and meals are available.

I first heard of Smith Island very early one morning in Manhattan's Fulton Street Fish Market. A rather effeminate gentleman, dressed somewhat inappropriately in light-colored slacks and suede shoes, tiptoed between upturned crates and dark puddles of melted ice. A fishhead peeped from the gutter. Tiny pink shrimp, still in their shells, lay crushed on the slippery sidewalk. Amid the hullabaloo of the market, the bawling of porters, the stench of tons of wet fish and the roaring of truck engines, the gentleman lectured a companion on the various forms of crustaceans displayed in the disheveled stands. "But the best—and I mean the very best—softshells are those delicious Smith Island creatures—buttery, smooth, they're impossible to describe, George, I mean they are just too gor-ge-ous for words!" He danced a little dance between the puddles and clapped his hands. "Our people love them. The darlings simply a-dore them." The man was ob-

Bay scene—Smith Island

viously a restaurateur—possibly he owned one of those elite New York restaurants where softshell crabs are featured as exorbitantly priced seasonal dishes. He certainly knew what he was talking about. Although famed Tangier Island surpasses Smith Island and every other part of Chesapeake Bay, for that matter, in crab catch, Smith is considered to produce the finest softshells in the region. Ask a Smith Islander: "Oh, my blessed, why, we got t'best bottoms, y'see, and we goes at it hard right from t'first rush" (the beginning of the season). "You got to read crabs right, but last year, oh, we was real smart o'crabs then. This year, why, it's slow. Toos many of them Jimmies just hang up on ye. But it'll be right, it'll be right—t'allus is, y'know."

One day I arrived on Smith Island. Somehow I knew I would. I love crabs; I also love to visit places that most people don't know exist. Tangier Island to the south (which I'll describe later) is becoming quite a popular excursion center, but there is only one ferry out to Smith and, except for a couple of busy summer weeks, it's often less than half full. Alan Tyler, captain of the *Betty Jo Tyler,* has no complaints. He lives in Rhodes Point, one of the three isolated communities on the island, and loves the place just as it is. During the winter his boat becomes the school bus, ferrying the older island children to the high school in Crisfield. "Only missed one day in the last two years. That's not bad, is it?" In the summer season he acts as skipper, guide and master of ceremonies for the small groups of visitors he carries daily to the island. On the journey over he talks about lunch at one of the island homes. When someone invariably asks for a rundown of the menu, Alan smiles and begins: "Weel, now, last I heard, Mrs. Evans was servin' softshells, crabcakes, clam fritters, oysters, fried fish, roast beef and ham—" (pause while a score of mouths begin to salivate) "—and y'dont have to choose. You get the lot, plus about a dozen vegetables, homemade biscuits and a few other surprises." Who could resist such regal fare? Well, I did, for one—foolishly. I was tempted, but wanted to explore the island. Actually there is plenty of time for both. I was a little wiser on my next visit.

The *Betty Jo Tyler* approached the island at a steady speed. It was flat, low-lying land. Clumps of trees scattered at irregular intervals along the marsh indicated isolated cottages in one of the three island communities. The choppy swell calmed as the boat entered a reed-lined cove. Herons, white egrets and ducks moved through the shallows. Warm breezes wafted the long grasses.

I chatted with a middle-aged man with bright, smiling eyes. His name was Lee Evans—one of scores of Evanses on the island, most of whom live in the community of Ewell (Rhodes Point is headquarters for the Tyler clan, and the more inaccessible Tylerton is home of the Bradshaws). "I'm really the black sheep. My brothers are all watermen. Dad was a great crabber, he could really read crabs— put me through school on the profits. That was my undoing. The island became too small for me. I love the people, although everyone knows what you're doing all the time." He laughed, "Folks on the mainland often wonder how a place like this works, with no government, no police, no jails. It's simple—everybody knows everything about everybody. It's like a family. If you want to live here, you've got to be one of them. An old black sheep like me still likes to come back. It's one of the nicest places I know."

The boat eased its way past the little crabbing shacks and the floating pounds where peeler crabs are kept until they shed their shells and can be packed off to market as fresh softs. As we nudged into dock, someone started up the engine of an old school bus and Captain Tyler announced we were going to take a brief tour of the island before lunch. There's one "road" across the marshes, about a mile long and full of bumps, linking Ewell to Rhodes Point. Even that is considered an example of excessive "modern'ty" by the older residents of Ewell. "Why in heck do we need a road for, just so's them Tylers can come into town once'n a while. They got boats. Better still, them bugs should fly 'em in." "Bugs" in this part of the world normally refers to those flying alligators the greenhead flies, which colonize the marshes during the hot months.

After much feuding between the residents the road was built and, as a result, the island became inundated with cars. Previously a few old trucks, salt-worn and held together by chunks of rust, supplied transportation needs. Today there's an amazing sight on the road to Rhodes Point. In the marsh is a line of abandoned automobiles, at least 100 of them, piled four and five high and stretching more than 100 yards. Captain Tyler, who was now driving the bus, seemed anxious to hurry past the eyesore "Well, y'know how it is. The sea air soon kills off a car." Some of them were recent models, no more than three years old. And now they sat in buckled and rusting glory, slowly being eaten away by the salt water. "There's talk of using 'em to protect the edges of the island," added the captain.

Apparently there's alarm at the rate the island is being eroded by the sea. Both Smith and Tangier Islands, according to early records, used to be twice the size they are today. There have been times recently when storms and unusually high tides have led to almost total inundation. Residents on nearby Holland Island had to move off some time back, and today only a tiny portion remains above water.

As Tylerton, at the southern end of Smith Island, is often inaccessible to the *Betty Jo Tyler* due to shallow tides, visitors (or "strange persons") spend most of their time in Ewell. It's a pleasant, unassuming little town. Behind the busy harbor filled with crabbing shacks, floats and all manner of Chesapeake fishing craft is the narrow, winding main street. The homes are simple Victorian-style structures, mainly white. Some still have exposed clapboard walls, but most have been re-sided. Fortunately, though, plastic pixies and similar garden trinkets have not yet made their appearance, and there's little evidence of wire mesh fencing here. Narrow oyster shell paths lead from the houses to the piers and crab pounds. Flags flutter in front yards, and a few tall trees cast welcome shade across the street. Inside the post office a group of older residents sit on straightback chairs

Street scene—Smith Island

and discuss island affairs. A blue station wagon with "U.S. Navy" stenciled in white on the side rushes past, driven by a young woman. "There goes Shim," remarks one of the ladies in the post office. "Lovely girl," says another; "Don't know what we'd do without her," adds a third. Shim Becker, an Australian, is the island nurse and seemingly is loved by everyone. "She's truly an angel of mercy, thank the Lord" says the owner of the general store near the harbor. Even Captain Tyler makes special mention of her house as we pass in the bus, and Bill Martin, editor and publisher of the *Crisfield Times,* claims that there have been few residents on Smith so cherished as Shim—"our nurse," as she is known locally.

The quiet, warm-hearted island of today, however, contrasts markedly with its past. Prior to the coming of Joshua Thomas, the "Preacher of the Islands" (see "Tangier Island"), Smith had a reputation for lawlessness, violence and drunkenness. Eking out a living from the sea was in those days a far less profitable and much more arduous business than it is today. The watermen worked hard and played hard. Family feuding was not uncommon. The spirit of independence was strong. When the Black and Jenkins Award of 1877 obliged Maryland to give 23,000 acres of high-quality oyster beds to Virginia (to help the Tangier fishermen), Smith Islanders went right on dredging in the area for more than 50 years until the beds ran out. There were regular fierce water battles; both sides lost men, but the "Smiths" refused to give in. Similarly, although the killing of wild ducks for market sale was outlawed in 1918, Smith Islanders continued to hunt the marshes, often using the deadly swivel guns that fired a pound of shot, killing or maiming a hundred ducks or more at a time. Some older residents still resent federal interference and claim that God has given them the abundant wildlife of the bay to be taken as they see fit. Even more recently many islanders bitterly resisted the attempted imposition of car licensing regulations and reacted against the creation of a wildlife refuge on a nearby marsh island. "Oh, my blessed, those govm't people, they cain't never leave nothin' the way t'is. Always snoopin' and passin' laws and messin' ev'body around." Yet, allowing for the occasional grumble, the islanders seem a happy and contented bunch. The Methodist churches are well attended, and the huge tabernacle in the center of Ewell supports large and enthusiastic camp meetings. The crab boats putter back into port during the summer with full bushel baskets, while the oyster boats bring in generous winter harvests.

There are signs of "modern'ty" like the recent introduction of telephones and microwave equipment and the surfacing of the Rhodes Point road. But the pace of life remains the same. The people speak with their traditional thick accent (occasionally it's impossible to decipher some of the more rapid exchanges between islanders). The quaint round-walled artesian wells are still the island's only water supply. The ducks and geese linger in the marshes on their long journey south, and Paul Marshall, over in Tylerton, still carves his famous wooden duck decoys. The hummocks in the marsh, full of the scent of pine and cedar, shade the homes of islanders. The crab shacks in the harbor provide the waterman with a quiet place of his own, somewhere between his home and the great gray-blue waters of the bay. The tourists haven't changed things that much. Smith is one of those places that just doesn't change easily.

12. WEST OCEAN CITY

This Maryland community is located south of the last traffic light on Route 50 before it crosses the bridge into Ocean City on the Atlantic coast.

"These people don't have to live here," the local official said in a tone verging on exasperation. "There's plenty of work around, especially in Ocean City during the summer. They just don't want to move. I suppose they've gotten used to it."

West Ocean City is not found on most maps. There are no road signs. Residents of adjoining communities pretend it's not there, and most visitors are not interested.

This tiny village of lopsided shacks is only one of scores of similar "barrios" found on the outskirts of prosperous towns throughout the Mid-Atlantic states. Sometimes the buildings are clustered cheek by jowl in a hollow away from the main road. Where land values are negligible they are scattered widely in reed-strewn fields. Lines of washing billow in the breeze; an old doorless refrigerator stands outside on the porch; junked cars, with trunks and hoods open wide like great butterfly wings, slowly rust in a swamp.

"We got this area on the priority list for fixin' up. How long? Well, it's hard to tell. Y'know how slow Washington is. Paperwork and more paperwork. Still, something should be done. Fire department came in last year and burnt down some of the worst places—just burnt 'em right down."

Only a hundred yards or so up the road from West Ocean City is the harbor. There's a lobstering fleet here—unusual on this part of the coast. Across from the trawlers is the marina, with about 60 private boats. Most cost around $70,000, but some much more.

Occasionally smoke from one of the shacks blows over the harbor and wafts through the tight riggings. The boat owners, tanned and dressed in crisp white shorts and socks, metal-rimmed sunglasses and jaunty captain's caps, continue polishing their brasswork, oblivious to life in the shanty town behind the reeds.

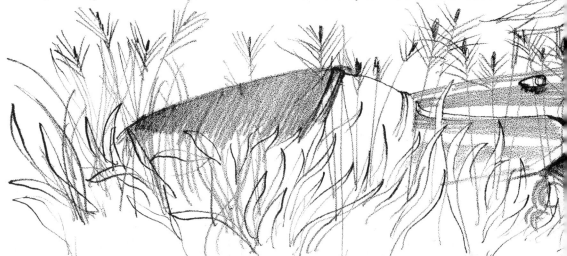

Marsh shacks—West Ocean City

13. TANGIER ISLAND

Crocketts, Pruitts and Dizes

Here's another Chesapeake Bay island, a little different from Smith but equally fascinating. Ferries run daily to Tangier Island from both Crisfield and Reedville (on the Virginia mainland side of the bay). The Crisfield Ferry normally leaves around 12:30 P.M. and returns at 5:00. The Reedville Ferry leaves at 10:00 A.M. and returns around 4:30. In both cases it is best to make reservations in advance during the summer (Crisfield: 804-891-2240; Reedville: 804-333-4656). Overnight accommodation and meals are available.

It all really began back in 1961. The distraught islanders were unable to find a doctor. Their previous physician had left and no one else seemed particularly anxious to take his place. So the mayor, Alva Crockett, decided it was time the world knew about their plight. At first their pleas warranted only a couple of columns in local newspapers. Then the *New York Times* picked the story up, and Alva and his town council were invited on televised talk shows to air their grievance. Although the publicity still didn't produce the needed permanent physician, the eyes of the nation were directed toward Tangier, and tourists—at least the more adventurous among them—came to explore this speck of land in the middle of Chesapeake Bay.

It certainly is a tiny place (and getting smaller as pieces slowly disappear into the sea), but that doesn't seem to worry the Tangiermen. They're much more concerned about their immediate livelihood, crabbing. In similar fashion to most other bay regions, the island has developed its own specialty, which, as gourmets well know, is the softshell crab. Actually it shares its reputation with Smith Island, but due to the long Virginia open season Tangier has a higher catch record than any other locality in the bay. It is equally well known for its winter "hard" crabs, caught by its dredger fleet. Yet at times visitors would hardly suspect that such a prolific industry existed here. During the day the harbor is calm; dinghies bob and bump against the wooden jetties, crab shacks are empty, groups of crab pounds lie still in the water. But early in the morning before dawn is a different matter. Then the village is filled with the racket of crackling engines as the host of little boats move into the bay; and late in the afternoon when they return there's a similar din, along with piles of bushel baskets filled with writhing, clicking, bubble-blowing blue crabs.

Most tourists never see this sight, unless of course they stay overnight at Mrs. Hilda Crockett's Chesapeake House. The majority only come for a couple of hours. But even they leave a little quieter in spirit, a little more relaxed—and possibly a little envious too.

This is still an idyllic place. Even though recent modernizations, including the widening of Main Street to a gross 10 feet, have introduced some insensitive vi-

Street scene—Tangier Island

Tangier Island

sual elements, life still continues much the way it did when the original settlers arrived in 1686. Prior to that time the only recorded European visitor to the area was Captain John Smith in 1608. During his brief exploration of the bay he also discovered and named Smith Island and, in typical fashion, wrote the following glowing account: ". . . a faire Bay compassed but for the mouth with fruitful and delightsome land. Within is a country that may have the prerogative over the most pleasant places of Europe, Asia, Africa or America, for large and pleasant navigable rivers. Heaven and earth never agreed better to frame a place for man's habitation." Obviously not many read or believed his words, as it was more than 150 years before the island developed anything of a real population. Most settlers came from Britain and many were related, hence the dominance today of such family names as Crockett, Parks, Pruitt, Dies (Dize) and Thomas. The confusion of family and first names has resulted in abundant use of nicknames and "tribal" references to different branches of the same family.

Although history is somewhat vague on the point, it is possible that life in those early days on the island was characterized by a considerable degree of lawless and licentious living, as was the case on nearby Smith Island. But then in 1804 along came Joshua Thomas in his boat *The Methodist,* bringing his great Bible full of lurid descriptions of the dreadful penalties awaiting the sinful residents of the islands. His bounding enthusiasm and stamina impressed the population, and in 1812, when he prayed with memorable results for a British defeat at Fort McHenry, he became the undoubted spiritual leader of Chesapeake Bay. The British, who had stationed themselves on Tangier prior to the battle and attended the service during which he forecast their rout, returned to the island to lick their wounds and marvel at the accuracy of Thomas' predictions.

Thomas is buried today in the churchyard of the Deal Island Methodist Church just across the bay, but his impact has remained. Tangier is a devoutly religious community. Work of any kind is still frowned upon on Sundays and church attendance is expected of everyone. Liquor of course is virtually nonexistent, and many of the small handwritten notices of forthcoming events found on store bulletin boards reflect the spiritual interests of the residents:

" 'The Gospel Of Jesus In Song' On Friday—Don't Miss It."

"Special Sunday School. Everybody welcome. Please Come On."

"The Gospel Boys Group Is Coming At Last—Should Be A Great Show!"

There's even a Volkswagen bus with a sign in large white letters: "Christ Is The Answer."

The island possesses a great sense of family unity. Until recently many front and back yards were used as family burial grounds. Study the headstones and note some of the unusual first names—Beaulah, Asbury, Sophronia, Dixie, Homer, Venie, Pettie.

Take your time here. There's no need to rush—unless of course you gorge yourself on one of Mrs. Crockett's huge lunches and walk the island, all within a couple of hours. Instead take a bicycle, the island's prime mode of transport, or there's the lazy way: little golf carts whose drivers offer guided tours around the island. Most of the young men who drive these machines do not speak with a real Tangier "olde English" accent. If they did you perhaps wouldn't understand one word of their commentary. Listen to the older residents speech— it's almost a foreign language, fascinating in the richness of its sound. There are touches of the Somerset and Cornish twangs and other ingredients not so readily identifiable, as well as words whose meanings have long since been forgotten by outsiders.

The main street, still with a few remnants of the once ubiquitous wooden fencing, is the highlight of the settlement. But it is also worth strolling across the marshes that stretch in a seemingly endless sweep of waving green grass down the length of the island. Cross the hump-backed bridges that leap over Big Gut Canal and visit the "outer" parts of the village. There are a few locally written guidebooks available that give fascinating background on the island. Frank Dize is normally near the pier when the ferry docks, selling copies of his *Something Fishy from Tangier* and his popular cookbook *Something Fishy from Tangier and Corny Too!* Vernon Bradshaw sells postcards of his own pencil sketchings in a tiny store near the Chesapeake House on Main Street. Occasionally visitors can also purchase softshells, crabcakes, clam fritters, diamondback terrapin and even locally grown figs to take back to the mainland.

The problem is, many people don't want to go back. According to Captain Evans, who runs the mailboat, a man from Pennsylvania recently purchased one of the little islands out in the harbor. How lovely it must be to have your own island . . .

Well, you can. Come to Tangier for a day or two, and you'll soon get that feeling that the island is yours to enjoy, any way you wish.

14. NORTHERN NECK
The Old Dominion

In addition to a proliferation of plantation mansions, churches, courthouses and other historical structures, the large peninsula in Virginia between the Potomac and Rappahannock Rivers, south of Washington, possesses a number of notable towns, including Farnham, Lancaster and Reedville.

The counties of Middlesex, Gloucester and Mathews on the adjoining peninsula have also been included with this region. These are less well-known areas and provide a pleasant contrast to the popular Northern Neck. Towns include Gloucester, Mathews, Deltaville, Port Haywood and Severn.

"Historyland," another name for Northern Neck, is a most appropriate title for this region. As a chronicler once wrote, "Here is the birth place of Washington, of Madison, of Monroe, of Thomas Marshall, father of John Marshall, of Richard Henry Lee and Francis Lightfoot Lee, signers of the Declaration of Independence, of General Robert E. Lee. Here are the ancestral homes of the Washingtons, the Balls, the Lees, the Carters, the Fitzhughs, the Fauntleroys, the Tayloes, the Monroes." The region has also been called "The Land of the Giants." In a less dramatic vein, Washington named it "The Garden of Virginia."

To attempt a description of all the historic sites and structures in Northern Neck is not the purpose of this chapter. Indeed the area is so well loved and so well marked that it hardly needs additional publicity. Visitors will easily find Washington's birthplace, Lee's birthplace, the Westmoreland State Park and other prominent sights without my help. Nevertheless there are little-known corners of the peninsula. But first, in order to fully appreciate the region, one must delve into its history and try to imagine the flavor and rhythm of the times when the land was still owned by notable English families, when slaves worked the wealthy plantations and sons of the gentry returned home from British schools in great masted sailing ships that docked at the tobacco wharves below the palatial riverside mansions. And which family better represents those times than the Carter clan, the wealthiest and most powerful of all Virginia landowners? It was dominated by the imposing presence of Robert "King" Carter, of whom it was once said, "If he failed at anything, no record of it remains."

John Carter settled on the banks of the Rappahannock River in the 1650s. Robert was born in 1663, and following the death of his father he inherited the estate and began to amass his fortune. As land agent for Lord Fairfax, proprietor of Northern Neck, Carter at one time or another occupied most of the positions of colonial power including speaker of the House of Burgesses, treasurer of the colony and acting governor. Over the years he acquired more than 300,000 acres of land, and when he died in 1732 he left behind him 14 children from two marriages, 1000 slaves and awesome wealth. His descendents included eight governors of

Christ Church—near Kilmarnock

Virginia, three signers of the Declaration of Independence, two Presidents (the Harrisons), a bishop, a chief justice and, not least, General Robert E. Lee.

Carter was by no means a modest man. To many he was a tyrant. To others he was a self-indulgent Royalist who ordered French and Madeira wines by the "pipe" (126 gallons) and English ale in 2000-bottle lots. He concentrated on tobacco production but traded in slaves as a lucrative sideline.

A permanent monument to Carter today is Christ Church, located near Kilmarnock at the southern tip of Lancaster County. This beautiful structure, modified Greek Cross in form, is said to be a virtual copy of Sir Christopher Wren's Farley Church in Wiltshire, England. It has brick walls more than three feet thick and is noted for its three-level "birdbox" pulpit and sounding board. Under a large headstone in the chancel is buried the father, John Carter, and four of his five wives (it was not unusual in those days for a man to be widowed several times, especially through childbearing). Outside by the wall of the church is the "King" 's own ornate tomb along with those of his two wives. Needless to say, this was really Carter's private church. He paid for it; his bricks were used to build it; he reserved more than a quarter of the pews for himself and his family and staff; he carried the key to open the doors on Sunday—and doubtless he advised the priest on the appropriateness of sermon topics.

In many ways he was a most progressive man for his time. He helped establish Virginia's flourishing economy, developed ports, built roads, pioneered new agricultural methods. He and his descendents left behind them a string of architec-

Sunnybank Ferry—near Reedville

tural gems—the Corotoman Mansion (only the site remains), the Shirley Mansion on the James River (see "Smithfield and Vicinity"), Sabine Hall in Richmond County and Nomini Hall (site only) in Westmoreland County. A biographer once wrote that "King" Carter made "so deep a mark upon his native tidewater Virginia that even today the people of the region talk about him as if he were still alive." It's true—they do. I met a group of ladies in the delightful library at Lancaster, situated on a lovely shaded green across from a colonnaded courthouse. They were involved in some genealogical research and were attempting to determine John Carter's birthplace in England. I listened to them discussing "King" Carter. They might have been talking about someone who lived just up the road, someone you might expect to see riding through the fields outside the town.

History is very real here, particularly to those local families whose ancestors were among the first settlers in the area. The "come-heres" (a disparaging term used to describe newcomers to Northern Neck) get a little tired of all these long lineages, though. "They're real snobs, y'know. If your family didn't come over with John Smith or one of those people, forget it. They don't want to know you." The young woman was particularly exasperated because a Bicentennial project she and some friends had tried to organize had flopped. "And do you know why? Because they said there were too many come-heres mixed up in it, and backed off. Now we can't even get the hall for a pageant. They've managed to spoil that too."

There are almost bound to be some bad feelings. The older families love the

Neck just as it was. They don't like changes. They fear the loss of a heritage—a traditional way of life. And it has nothing to do with wealth: some of the well-to-do families at Reedville and Fleeton, for example, living in extravagant Victorian mansions, are regarded by many to be just as much come-heres as the poorer immigrants, in mobile homes or shacks on the edge of a cornfield. The Reedville residents, though, don't seem to mind too much and continue to make fortunes from the processing of menhaden fish in the harbor facing Chesapeake Bay. At one time during the 1940s this was the richest town per capita in the country. It retains that appearance today. The purse seine fishing fleet is one of the best equipped in the world. More than a half billion pounds of oil-filled menhaden are caught annually, which makes this tiny port the nation's number-one fishing center (and, much to the chagrin of New England fishermen, makes Virginia the second most important fin fish state in the nation). A large proportion of the catch is processed for fish meal, oil and cat food, but over a third is sold to the watermen of the bay for crab bait.

It's the smaller villages and tiny country churches that give Northern Neck much of its real character and traditional charm. At Mount Holly, on a hill just above the highway (Route 202), is the simple, white-painted Nomini Church, originally founded in 1704. A later renovation was burned by the British during one of their frequent pillaging expeditions in the area during the War of 1812. Not content with destroying the church, the invaders also stole the silverplate. It was not until 1848 that the church was rebuilt.

A few miles to the south is one of the most historic churches in America, Yeocomico Church. Originally built in 1655, today's structure dates from 1706. It too suffered at the time of the Revolution and in the 1812 war, when the communion table was used by His Majesty's troups as a chopping block and the marble font as a wine holder. Today restoration is complete and the little church, with its brick floor, white woodwork and "slaves' gallery," is open to the public on a regular basis.

On the south side of the peninsula near Lively is one of my favorite churches, St. Mary's White Chapel. It sits tiny and sedate among trees and tombs, looking more like a small cottage than a church. It's not too well known and is a lovely place to spend a quiet hour or so when exploring the area.

For those travelers who like to ride little-known river ferries (and judging by the volume carried on the Woodland Ferry near Seaford, Delaware, it's a popular hobby), there are two worthy of note. The first is at Sunnybank, near Reedville. According to the sign, full of rather complex instructions about buttons and bells, it operates free of charge from 7 A.M. to 7 P.M. every day except Sunday. The second is located to the south at Merry Point, serving the villages of Ottoman and Bertrand. Neither really leads anywhere in particular, but they give access to some lovely back roads along the Potomac and Rappahannock Rivers.

Let's go south across the Rappahannock and travel some narrow lanes around the county towns of Gloucester and Mathews. Here we find a gently rolling landscape of forests and cornfields. Tobacco, once plentiful in this area, is not so evident today, but in the charming riverside village of Urbanna there's an old tobacco warehouse (c. 1763) on Prettyman's Rolling Road. Farther up the Mattaponi and Pamunkey Rivers to the west the forests thicken and intermingle with swamplands and marshes. The rivers were named after local Indian tribes, and two reservations are still maintained today along their banks, with trading posts open to the public.

The Mathews Peninsula is a little world unto itself. The town of Mathews possesses a charming courthouse complex—court, clerk's office, county offices, library and jail all set in a minicampus of trees and lawns just off Main Street. This layout is quite typical of the Northern Neck area. Lancaster and the towns of King and Queen have similar arrangements, and particularly memorable is the courthouse historic district in Gloucester.

A few miles to the north of Mathews is Gwynn's Island, where according to local legend a grave was dug for Captain John Smith after he had an encounter with a stingray at nearby Deltaville which was assumed, incorrectly, to be fatal. Smith seems to have been a very lucky man.

A few miles to the south near the village of Hayes a rough path leads to "Powhatan's Chimney," supposedly the place where the eleven-year-old Pocahontas saved Smith's life. It was an Indian custom that a person thus saved was given to his protector, but Smith also managed to avoid that entanglement and left Chief Powhatan's daughter for John Rolfe (see "Smithfield and Vicinity").

Gloucester Court House

To the east of Mathews, along one of the many narrow lanes that meander over the peninsula, is the restored 1879 Methodist Tabernacle. Revivals are still a familiar occurrence in the Tidewater, and at the time of my visit I saw posters for a July camp meeting. Just a little farther up the road there's a second tabernacle, supposedly used on rare occasions by Quakers.

Roam around the peninsula at will. Even the unpaved back roads ultimately lead to blacktop, so it's almost impossible to get lost. I found tiny oyster creeks with boats of bushel baskets littering the old wooden piers; I had a snack at a local soul food restaurant, J. B.'s Chick and Fin; I sketched the post office at Shadow— surely one of the smallest in Virginia; I explored deserted mansions and discovered what once must have been slave shacks.

Farther to the south I ventured into an area known as Guinea on the Severn Peninsula. Once this was dangerous territory for outsiders—no one was welcome after dark. Today, though, it looks pleasant enough. There are some unusual shack communities on the back roads and I spotted evidence of mongoloid features remindful of Appalachia, but for the most part it seems a clean, well-kept area. Its proximity to the Norfolk–Newport News–Hampton Roads urban area possibly accounts for a smattering of overpretty commuter cottages.

To the south the Poquoson area, which once had an equally notorious reputation, is being swamped by suburbia. All that remains is Big Island out in the bay. There's a mystery to this place. It's privately owned and visitors are not welcome. Mainland residents tell stories of snoopers disappearing without trace. It's hard to separate fact from fiction here but most locals prefer to leave the island's strange inhabitants in peace. There are ghosts too—the old pine woods near Mathews are said to hide the spirits of murdered Royalists and pirates killed in a drunken brawl. Occasional reports are also heard of ghost ships just off the coast.

The people whose families have been here for generations just smile and nod knowingly as these tales are related. The come-heres and hidden-corners travelers are the ones who get intrigued by the mysteries of this fascinating region.

Tabernacle—near Mathews

Small plantation mansion—near Smithfield

15. SMITHFIELD AND VICINITY
Pork and Peanuts in Southside

Many visitors to Jamestown and Williamsburg, Virginia, look for a little respite from overorganized itineraries. Across the James River is another world—a little touch of Dixie—a region of pine forests, peanut fields, hog farms and peaceful living. There's hunting, history, fishing, fine cuisine at old inns, even a pleasant seaside resort to end the journey. Communities within the area include Surry, Smithfield, Wakefield, Wallaceton and Back Bay.

The best way to enter Southside is by the Jamestown Ferry, which many visitors to the Williamsburg-Jamestown area are unaware exists. It's a short journey across the brown water. The hurly-burly of the Williamsburg crowd is soon left behind. The boat nudges its way into the wharf at Scotland on the other side, and after the cars roll off and up the hill all is quiet. A heron circles and lands, legs a-gaggle, in the reeds at the edge of the water. Something beige and furry scurries across the road.

In the window of the local store there's a roughly printed handbill. It reads: "Surry's Pork, Peanut And Pine Festival," and goes on to describe some of the promised delights: displays of the area's three primary industries—pork raising and packing, peanut farming, and lumbering; musical entertainment by the Goochland County Band and the Hampton Lion's Club Jug Band, and finally a listing of epicurean delights to be served at the festival—barbecued whole pig, spareribs, ham and redeye gravy, chitlins, ham biscuits, cracklin' cornbread, peanut soup, peanut pie, peanut cookies, peanut brittle, spiced and sugared peanuts, etc.

Unfortunately I was two days late. The festival had come and gone.

Both banks of the James River between Newport News and Richmond are littered with old fort sites, mansions, manor houses and churches, reflecting the days when rivers were the highways of the young nation. On the north side particularly, along Route 5, the names resound with history. Shirley, the legendary plantation home of the Carter family (see "Northern Neck") since 1723; Berkeley, ancestral home of Presidents William Henry Harrison and Benjamin Harrison; Sherwood Forest, home of President John Tyler, and finally Carter's Grove, built by "King" Carter's grandson between 1750 and 1753 and claimant to the title of "Most Beautiful House in America."

Southside is equally well endowed with places of historic interest. Not far from Petersburg is the Merchant's Hope Church, said to have been completed in 1657. This rather austere rectangular structure is one of the oldest Protestant churches still standing in America and continues in use as a house of worship. A little farther to the east, a few miles north of Route 10 on Route 611, is Brandon, a mansion of exquisite simplicity set high above a wide expanse of river. The land here was once owned by Richard Quiney, brother of Thomas Quiney, who married William Shakespeare's daughter. In common with many of the plantation homes along the James, it was bombarded by the British during the Revolutionary era and later suffered at the hands of Union forces during the Civil War.

Continuing eastward, there's Claremont Manor, set in magnificent grounds alongside the James. How these early plantation owners must have lived—surrounded by flourishing tobacco fields, served regularly by sailing ships bringing luxuries from Europe in exchange for hogsheads of dried tobacco, amply supplied with livestock, slaves, game from the nearby forests—they must have felt like little princes or, in the case of "King" Carter, almost regal monarchs in their own right.

One of the more modest historical buildings in the area is to be found just south of the ferry wharf at Scotland. This is Smith's Fort Plantation House, better known as the Rolfe or Warren House. The land was originally a gift from Chief Powhatan to John Rolfe in 1614 on the occasion of Rolfe's marriage to his daughter, Pocahontas. A few years previously, in 1609, Captain John Smith had erected a fort nearby to safeguard Jamestown from the Indians and the Spanish. Later the plantation was inherited by Rolfe's son Thomas, who subsequently sold it to Warren. Warren built a house here in 1652; the present structure is said to date from 1720. (It was restored in 1935 by the Association for the Preservation of Virginia Antiquities.)

East of Smith's Fort are two additional places of interest. The beautiful Chippokes State Park has been an active plantation for over 300 years. Within the 1400-acre grounds is a fine example of an antebellum mansion, completed in 1856. Nearby, just off Route 10, is the unusual Bacon's Castle. Situated at the end of a wide avenue of ancient maples, the house was originally constructed in 1655 by a Britisher, Arthur Allen, who came to America to escape a turbulent love affair. It combines some Tudor architectural features, most notably the tall, clustered chimney stacks, with more conventional window and door detailing. The unfortunate Mr. Allen experienced a second trauma when some of Nathaniel Bacon's rebels commandeered the mansion in 1676 during the notorious Bacon's Rebellion. Many Northerners have forgotten this early revolt against British tyranny, but not the Southerners. They revere the memory of Nat Bacon's courage and endurance.

He was a young man, recently educated at Oxford, when he set out for America in 1673. His learning and manners soon secured him a seat in the Virginia Council, and a year later he was embroiled in a feud with Charles II's British governor, Sir William Berkeley. It appears that Berkeley was ineffective in preventing destructive raids upon the settlers by the Susquehanna and Occoneechee Indians, so Bacon formed his own defensive militia. Berkeley immediately declared Bacon "the greatest rebel that ever was in Virginia," although a direct confrontation was avoided when Bacon was elected to a new Council and duly pardoned. But that was not the end of the matter. The proud Bacon, hearing that Berkeley was plotting against him, regrouped his rebels, forced the governor to evacuate the area

and, as virtual head of the government, persuaded the Council to liberalize the stringent laws of the colony. Berkeley returned but Bacon stormed Jamestown, chased the poor governor out again and issued a proclamation threatening Virginian independence. Then, suddenly, he died of a fever. Berkeley hanged more than 20 "rebels" without trial, then was summoned back to England, where he passed away within a year. But the Virginians continued to revolt. In 1683 there were tobacco riots all along the Tidewater region. Only in 1689, when James II was expelled and William and Mary took over the throne, did a semblance of peace return to the troubled colony.

But that's all history—important, especially if one is to appreciate the true character of this part of the Tidewater, but history nonetheless. Let's move farther down Route 10 to the town of Smithfield and discuss something a little more tangible. Hams! Hams today are big business. Upwards of $90 million flows into the town each year from the sales of the three major companies, Gwaltney, Smithfield Packing and Spriggs.

It all began really with Cato the Elder in 149 B.C. He described the step-by-step process of curing hams in his *De Re Rustica,* and today, more than 2100 years later, the Smithfield method still follows Cato's principles. Hundreds of hams hang in the smokehouses at the edge of town, and fragrant aromas are a perpetual reminder of Smithfield's primary source of income.

If you've never tasted real Smithfield ham you're in for a treat. Queen Victoria loved it, and export records go back to the 1770s. Go to the Old Smithfield Inn on

Country scene in Southside

Main Street, built in 1752 (about the same time that the curing process was being refined), for a ham dinner. Preceded by an appetizer of Brunswick Stew (without the traditional squirrel meat) and cornbread biscuits, there are few gourmet delights to match a thinly sliced glowing-red Smithfield. (My mouth waters as I write.)

Before you leave, take a stroll around the town. There are some resplendent Victorian houses on the steep bluff above the river and past the inn is the old Isle of Wight Courthouse (1751), featuring an arcaded porch and rounded brick courtroom. Nearby is the county jail, dating from the late 1700s, and the county museum.

A few miles south of town on Route 10 is St. Luke's Church ("Old Brick"), one of the most beautiful in the region and reminiscent of a typical English parish church. Inside, the communion table and chairs are rare examples of fine seventeenth-century American craftsmanship. Substantial restoration was required in the 1880s but there is considerable evidence to support the claim that this is an original 1632 structure.

Departing Smithfield, take a drive into the real Southside. Leave the stately James River behind and drift southward along country lanes through a beautiful landscape of forests, cornfields and peanut plantations. Abandoned farms and barns lean precariously, supported by sinews of ivy or a solitary brick chimney. A group of elderly blacks sit on the reeded banks of a pond fishing with homemade bamboo poles. Occasionally, down long, dusty tracks between cornfields, there is a glimpse of an old plantation mansion. On a telephone pole a sign reads: "A Great Holy Ghost Revival—Bring The Sick And All Who Need Help." Outside a gas station there's another sign: "Muskrats for Sale."

It's a quiet land. The pace of life seems slow, in tune with the steady change of seasons. Large, lopsided general stores, half empty inside, brood on silent main streets. Farther south there are the tobacco fields. In Mecklenburg County thoroughbreds were once raised on the great plantations.

To the east is a very different kind of landscape around an area known as the Great Dismal Swamp. This is a strange, silent wilderness. Thomas Moore, the Irish poet, wrote his famous "Lake of the Dismal Swamp" after a visit here in 1903. Harriet Beecher Stowe and Longfellow also used the swamp as a setting in their works. Unfortunately, due to a diminishing water table and the gradual encroachment of cornfields, it's difficult to get anything but infrequent glimpses into the gloomy cypress tunnels that penetrate the wilderness, one of the last of its kind in America. On the eastern side, though, near Wallaceton, Alva Duke runs regular boat tours to Lake Drummond in the heart of the swamp along one of the many canals that crisscross the mire. (The first major canal was developed by George Washington—he owned land in the swamp and wanted to provide a convenient way to harvest and transport the magnificent stands of cypress and oak.) It's a trip that visitors long remember.

Alva Duke is one of the swamp's most fervent admirers. He has written books, appeared before government committees, helped formulate legislation, all in a desperate bid to save the area from impending annihilation. Mr. Duke claims that the illegal draining of the swamp is reducing the water level to such a point that a subterranean peat fire would be virtually impossible to douse and would eventually reduce the whole area to "a sacrificial funeral pyre," killing every tree and every species of wild animal within its boundaries. I hope his efforts to draw attention to this immediate dilemma will prove successful.

Having journeyed as far as this, fellow hidden-corners seekers should perhaps indulge themselves in a little luxury and continue eastward to the coast. Around Currituck Sound and Back Bay is quiet hunting and fishing country—and to the north is Virginia Beach herself. Even though plagued by the jets from the adjoining naval air station, it's a clean and pleasant ocean resort, a perfect place to end a slow journey through Southside.

The Mountain Region

16. BLAIRSTOWN AND VICINITY
A Small-Town Bicentennial

On the northern New Jersey border, bounded by the Delaware River east of the Poconos, is this delightfully secluded corner full of quiet valleys and narrow country lanes. I saw a small town at play here during its Bicentennial celebration. I also found places like Peters Valley, Belvidere, Delaware, Millbrook and Hope—an old Moravian village whose founders were too honest to make a living.

The banner across the road read: "Blairstown Bicentennial Celebration." It was only 11 A.M. but Frank's Place, the small roadside tavern a block away from Main Street, was already awash in peanut shells floating in frothy pools of spilled beer. The interior was packed with customers so Frank set up an impromptu extension outside complete with folding tables and refrigerator. Business was brisk.

Mayor Ben Fodera felt he had already been going a whole day. He had risen early to check last-minute preparations with members of the Bicentennial Committee. There was concern about the weather—dark clouds hung over the town. Tony Fowler the park chairman was disgruntled: "After all our efforts, why does it have to go'n be like this?"

At 11 Mayor Fodera was dedicating the new Foot Bridge Park ("A Quiet Place") on the site of the Blair Railroad marshaling yard by Paulins Kill. Then the crowds, growing larger by the minute, deluged the Presbyterian hall for a lunch of hoagies and sloppy joes served by the ladies of the town. Woodrow Houck, another member of the committee, strode majestically between the tables in silk breeches, wig, walking cane and three-cornered hat. Outsiders, not quite caught up in the spirit of the occasion, gave him strange glances. Children giggled. One little girl, her mouth dribbling with sloppy joe, gurgled, "Who's that man, mummy? Why's he wearing those funny—" Mother clapped her hand over the little girl's mouth with such force that the sloppy joe went flying in all directions. A drip landed on poor Woodrow's blue velvet coat. He looked down, tried to flick it off with his finger but only managed to spread it around more. He smiled a sickly smile at the mother and retired with dignity to an adjoining dining room set aside for officials.

Around 1 P.M. the pet show began in the town hall car park. A couple of thousand visitors strained over each other's shoulders to catch a glimpse of the exhibits. The prize categories were endless: prettiest cat, smartest dog, largest pet, smallest pet, even prizes for the pet owner who had traveled farthest to be at the Blairstown Celebration.

The final award was for the most unusual pet. There was a goat dressed in a Bicentennial outfit, a goose swathed in ribbons and bows, pet mice painted red, white and blue, a tortoise who never once showed his face, a pet seahorse in a glass bowl, a chipmunk who slept throughout the proceedings and a small alligator, its jaws tightly tied with string, lying in a shoebox. The little boy, who was its owner explained the alligator's apparent lack of movement: "He's scared." The reptile didn't look scared though—it peered at the spectators through tiny black eyes and seemed to be wishing the string around its jaws would snap so it could take a good healthy bite out of those irritating youngsters who kept poking it with their fingers.

After much careful deliberation, the alligator received first prize. That didn't improve its mood in the least. "I don't think he likes it here," the little boy said as he clamped the lid on the shoebox and walked off with the award. The little girl with the fancy goose cried to her mother, "Mine is best, mine is best!" The goose was unconcerned. It started to eat a pile of raffle tickets left on a table. The lady selling them bawled, "Who's going to pay for the ones he's eaten?" The child became even more upset: "It's not his fault, it's not his fault!" The mother led her away dragging the reluctant goose wrapped in ribbons. "We should never have come," she muttered. "It was your father's stupid idea."

By midafternoon the crowd was getting restless. A short rainstorm had left everyone looking a little damp as the celebrants began lining Main Street to watch the big parade. Street vendors wheeled shopping carts full of Bicentennial junk: inflatable Mickey Mouses and 747s, striped balloons, flags, whistles, ceramic mugs, caricature models of Nixon, even White House brochures and lapel buttons with sexy captions.

The parade began promptly at 4 P.M. The rain held off for a while, and as parades go it was a most impressive effort. There were police floats, fire brigades, displays by local hospitals, marching columns of boy scouts, guides, the national guard, all kinds of volunteer organizations, a clever exhibit by a local Moravian school. A line of past and present automobiles drove by, following a pair of magnificent Clydesdales that towed the complete Bicentennial Committee perched on a beer wagon. Amzi Linaberry, the town's oldest resident, waved to the cheering crowd from an antique car.

At Frank's Place the beer continued to flow. The "when you've seen one, you've seen 'em all" crowd were crammed four deep around the bar. Over at the school a square-dancing exhibition was in progress. The skydiving performance scheduled for 6 P.M. was canceled due to low clouds, and there was some doubt about holding the much-heralded Bicentennial fireworks extravaganza later on in the evening.

One show everyone wanted to see was the band concert at the high school. The auditorium was full as the American Weldery and Steel Band pounded out its marching tunes. Sousa would have been proud of it. For almost two hours the players never flagged, and the audience loved it. They even remained for the speeches. Then they moved reluctantly out into the rainy night, disappointed about the postponed fireworks display. "Well, it's almost over," one of the Bicentennial Committee wives murmered to her husband. She adjusted her Marie Antoinette wig as he straightened his canary-yellow breeches.

"Yep, I'm tired."

"Do you think they enjoyed it?" she asked.

"Who knows?" he replied. Then he smiled. "I know I did," he said and led her to the car, twirling his sword with its silver handle.

The affair at Blairstown was just one of hundreds, maybe thousands, of similar events that took place all over the country during 1976. The Bicentennial itself didn't seem to be the important factor. It was more of an excuse for communities to have fun together, to express pride in what they have and what they are, to enjoy the conviviality of neighbors and strangers alike. It also gave many towns an opportunity to reflect on their own heritage. In the case of Blairstown, by the time that John I. Blair, the Lackawanna Railroad millionaire, had his special railroad laid to the town in 1876, his Blair Academy was famous throughout the East and the town was becoming an attractive summer resort for Philadelphians. Even the grisly antics of the Blairstown murderess Martha Place, the first woman to die by the electric chair in America, in no way detracted from the town's popularity. It has changed little since those days. Just above Main Street the mill pond forms the heart of a delightful park, perfect for picnics. The old stone mill, arched over the sidewalk, still dominates Main Street. There's an almost western flavor here reminiscent of the Sierra towns of California. Many of the wooden buildings have large second-floor porches over rambling stores. There's a bar and liquor store

with all the atmosphere of a gold-rush saloon, and steps lead from raised sidewalks into the street. All the town needs are a few tie rails for horses and a sturdy hanging tree to complete the illusion.

Of course, there was a time when this was real frontier territory. The lord proprietors of New Jersey, in an effort to encourage settlement of the rolling hills along the Delaware River, promised 150 acres to every freeman who could furnish "a gold musket, bore twelve bullets to the pound, with bandoliers and match convenient and with six months' provisions for himself." In the early 1700s much of the labor of clearing forest and cultivating the land was undertaken by slaves and "redemptioners." The latter were normally Europeans who sold themselves for an agreed period of years in return for the price of their passage to America. They often fared little better than the slaves. Records in the Blairstown Library (housed in the Old Mill) tell of Philadelphia auctions in 1722 where German redemptioners were sold at $50 each for five years of committed servitude.

Settlement in the area can be traced to the Dutch, who as far back as 1650 built a road to carry ore from their Pahaquarry copper mine to Esopus (Kingston) on the Hudson. Some remains of these mines can still be seen today near Walpack Center, and sections of Route 521 along the Delaware, south from Montague, follow the Old Mine Road, originally more than 100 miles long.

During the French and Indian War (see "Honesdale and Vicinity") and later, during the Revolutionary era, the area was constantly under attack by Indians. Mini-

sink Island in the Delaware was the home of the Wolf Clan of the Leni Lenape, and the famous Minisink Trail to the sea originated here. A chain of seven forts was constructed along the river to protect the settlers, but such conflicts as the Swarthout Massacre in 1755 and the battle with Brant's Indians in 1780 near Montague occurred regularly. Historic markers along the Old Mine Road tell these tales.

The drive over the river foothills below Stokes State Forest and the Appalachian Trail is one of the most interesting and beautiful in northern New Jersey. Start at Montague in the north or at the Water Gap to the south and follow the river road, taking side trips at random. If you fancy yourself a canoeist, cross the Delaware at Dingmans Ferry (a private toll bridge) and rent one of the boats at the office by the restaurant. Alternatively, if you're interested in crafts, follow the narrow road to the "funky oasis" at Peters Valley, a tiny village set in the hills east of the river. The old store at the crossroads has been converted into a crafts shop displaying the varied works of artisans who live and practice their skills in the many local studios. Funding comes from the National Park Service, and crafts courses are held "to stimulate the appreciation of contemporary crafts as an art form and as an expression of our American culture." It's a place full of life and activity, offering resident programs for professional craftsmen, internship programs, weekend workshops and a range of summer sessions in such areas as ceramics, blacksmithing, loom tapestry, photography, plastics, dyeing and weaving, "found-object" jewelry, appliqué, woodcarving, basketry and metal sculpture. The day I visited, students were gathering at the large white house behind the store for a "show 'n' tell" session at the end of a series of courses. There was a lovely spirit to the place. Everyone looked bright-eyed and enthused by the whole experience. The handicrafts reflected an integrity of learning and skill, a pride in quality of the work. Outsiders are welcome and the studios are always open to the public. It's a most refreshing place.

Down the road a little way, at Millbrook, is another village developed by the National Park Service which will ultimately become a restored colonial settlement, with a hotel, gristmill, blacksmith's forge, shoemaker's shop, store and cider press. Whether it in turn will be part of a much larger recreational area linked to the proposed Tocks Island Dam and the Foothills Freeway, is open to question. The proposal is still alive but so far no funds have been authorized. Residents are confused. Summer cottages and riverside lands have been abandoned. There's an air of frustrated expectancy in the region, and both sides in the controversy are sharpening their weapons, ready for a renewal of skirmishes.

It's hard to imagine conflict in this lovely corner of New Jersey where villages slumber in quiet valleys. Along the hill road out of Peters Valley there's an old stone building, the Van Campen Inn (c. 1750), where Vice President John Adams was hosted. It looks over a scene of rolling hills and forests that has changed little in two centuries. Even where change has taken place and the brash world of gas stations and truck stops asserts itself, on Route 46 near the Water Gap, the Victorian village of Delaware, set back from the road, retains its total composure and gentility.

Belvidere, seat of Warren County, also possesses an air of distinction, especially around the park, with its courthouse, four churches and stately homes. There are some lovely riverside drives in this area through Roxburg Station and Harmony, and if you enjoy mountain rides try the back roads over Scotts Mountain leading to Washington, Oxford and Butzville. These are all particularly memorable in the fall season.

The village of Hope, to the north, reflects the attraction the New Jersey and Pennsylvania mountains once had for religious and other socially distinct groups (see "Coudersport to New Milford"). Here, on the top of a steep hill, a group of Moravians from the mother colony at Bethlehem settled in 1774. They built a sturdy stone community including mills, an inn, a brewery and a distillery. Most of the buildings still remain today, and there's a romantic tale about the gristmill, down the hill from the stores. It appears that the son of a local farmer took a fancy to the miller's daughter, but the miller, who lived on the first floor of his establishment, forbade any meetings between them. The young people devised a scheme whereby the daughter, who was used to hauling heavy sacks of flour to the top floor by pulley, hauled up her lover instead. The story goes on: "While the miller was innocently attending to his duties on the first floor, the young couple were

Valley scene—near Hope

worshipping at the altar of Cupid on the fourth." According to the writer it all ended satisfactorily—the miller was reconciled to the union, and the couple became "useful and respected citizens."

Unfortunately, the story of Hope didn't end quite so happily. A smallpox epidemic killed many settlers in the early 1800s, and there were other problems too according to the official Warren County history: "The Moravians were a remarkably honest set of people . . . but by trusting too much in the honesty of those with whom they transacted business, they suffered in their pecuniary affairs and in 1805 or 06 abandoned their Hope enterprise and returned to Bethlehem."

Make a special effort to visit Hope. Not only is it one of the most attractive villages in this part of New Jersey but it reflects the great determination and dedication of early religious settlers. The Moravians could have built clapboard homes, but instead they used stone. They could have selected a level site but chose a hill. They could have compromised their values and made a healthy profit from their trading, but they refused to do so even when others cheated them. Their pioneering project inevitably failed, but the village remains as testimony to their spirit. Hope is appropriately named.

17. THE MERCER MILE: DOYLESTOWN

Doylestown, Pennsylvania, is located on Route 611 approximately 30 miles north of Philadelphia.

Perhaps more than any other western nation, America has during its relatively short history encouraged enthusiastic individuality of expression on the part of its citizens. Occasionally this attitude has manifested itself in structural forms, and on my travels I am continually looking for the odd, the unusual and the unique in architectural vernaculars. Regrettably, the Mid-Atlantic states seem relatively devoid of freakish forms, possibly due to their stringent colonial origins or the subsequent rigors of the economic climate. So, imagine my delight when I arrived one day in Doylestown and found not one but three of the most incredible structures, all within a mile of each other and all the work of a single, and singular, gentleman—Dr. Henry Chapman Mercer.

Dr. Mercer (1856–1930) was a true "Renaissance man," knowledgeable and skilled in many fields and fascinated by the richness of life itself. As a young man he practiced law in Philadelphia, but later he pursued his interests in archeology and anthropology. He wrote extensively. He assembled vast collections of agricultural and crafts implements. He was appointed a curator at the University of Pennsylvania museum; he led explorations and "digs"; he was associate editor of the *American Naturalist.* He was also fascinated by ceramics and gained fame as a manufacturer of magnificently decorative tiles based on widely divergent influences, including Pennsylvania German, ancient Anglo-Saxon and Aztec designs and motifs. He eventually designed and constructed his Moravian Pottery and Tile Works (1910–12), which is still in operation today.

But the creation for which he is best known is his Fonthill Mansion (1908–10), at the eastern edge of Doylestown (open Wednesday through Sunday, 10 A.M. to 3:45 P.M.). Dr. Mercer, an "American Gaudi", was one of the first builders ever to use reinforced concrete, and by designing from the inside out was a precursor of contemporary architectual theory. Tiles of every kind adorn each room, corner and niche. Dr. Mercer described his concept as follows: "The plan of the whole house was an interweaving of my own fancies blending with memories of my travels and suggestions from several engravings [and] a woodcut illustrating a story called 'haunted.' " I won't even begin to describe the intricacies and the surprises of this place. The sketches capture some of its spirit, but the only way to appreciate it is to go through it. And while in Doylestown visit Dr. Mercer's third structure, the Mercer Museum (Tuesday through Sunday, 10 A.M. to 5 P.M.), home of his unique collection of 30,000 domestic agricultural and crafts artifacts—"the tools of the nation maker."

Try to allow a whole day for exploring the mansion, the museum and the tile works. If you have more time, enjoy a stroll through the side streets of this lovely

Fonthill Mansion—Doylestown

hilltop town (follow the bike route) and then go on to travel through the surrounding countryside of Bucks County. Parts are becoming a little too tourized for most hidden-corners explorers, but there's still plenty of interest here, particularly along the Delaware Canal and around the villages of New Hope and Fallsington. The upper section of the county around Dublin is quieter and equally scenic.

Mercer creations

18. HONESDALE AND VICINITY
Glimpses of Young America

It's hard to believe these quiet hills have such a long and varied history. This was once tough frontier territory, and tales of Indian raids and massacres are familiar.

The region is located east of Scranton, Pennsylvania, and is bounded on the north by Route 371, on the south by 84, on the east by the Delaware River and on the west by the mountain range above Carbondale. Towns include Honesdale, Hawley, Lackawaxen, Bethany and South Canaan.

Except for the occasional canoe enthusiast racing through the whitewater of the Delaware River, the valleys east of Honesdale are tranquil places. Resort cottages are scattered in the mountains around Greeley (see "Coudersport to New Milford"), but they're hidden in the forest and in no way detract from the charm of the region.

It hasn't always been like this. During the French and Indian War and Revolutionary period, settlers in these hills were constantly harassed by Indians and their white allies. It took tough men and women to scrabble for a living here. The valleys were steep-sided, fertile soil was limited and communication with the outside world rare and fleeting. Later when coal was discovered in the Scranton-Carbondale area, it took an equally sturdy breed to work down the damp shafts and to construct the sinews of canals and railroads for hauling the "black diamonds" to the large East Coast cities.

Today we may be attracted by the wilderness of the region, its tiny valleys and racing streams. But there's much more here. Maybe as we look at the area's history we will appreciate its true character a little more.

I paused at Minisink Ford on the New York side of the Delaware above Port Jervis. Stretching across the river was a most unusual bridge—a minisuspension affair with a wooden causeway built on huge stone piers. The piers looked totally disproportionate to the width of the bridge. I spoke with a man at the tollgate shack, and he pointed out the bronze landmark plaque, which tells that here there was originally an aqueduct canal, built in 1848 for the Delaware and Hudson Coal Company as part of the system linking the anthracite fields beyond Honesdale with Kingston on the Hudson River. Sections of the canal followed the Old Mine Road built by the Dutch in the 1650s, which also terminated at Kingston (see "Blairstown and Vicinity"). The railroad eventually superseded the canal, and the aqueduct was purchased privately and converted into a suspension bridge. Its creator was none other than John A. Roebling, designer of the Brooklyn Bridge, and it is thought to be the oldest suspension-type structure still standing in the United States.

Up the steep hill beyond the bridge on the New York side (this region is full of steep hills) is a small park, hidden from the road and ignored by most visitors. It's worth the drive and the walk, even farther up the mountain, to visit the site of an infamous massacre here in 1779. The story is told on tape; press the button near the flagpole and you'll learn much about the continual conflicts of settlers and Indians in those early days. The French during the French and Indian War began to form alliances with local tribes and to attack mountain settlers, who, they claimed, were encroaching westward upon their territory.

Eventually the French threat was eradicated by a combined British and colonial army, but as the Revolution approached, conflicts in the area began again. This time it was Tories, loyal to the Crown, who formed alliances with the local tribes and encouraged them to attack the rebellious settlers. The Indians needed little persuasion. They had seen how the colonialists had broken treaties and stolen lands at will. They attacked settlers throughout the mountain region. One such attack, led by the infamous Tory Joseph Brant, was the Minisink incident mentioned previously.

On July 22, 1779, 150 settlers and members of the militias of New York and New Jersey, under a Major Wood, decided to ambush the raiders on their return up the river from an attack to the south. However, they were themselves outnumbered and massacred on the rocky summit of the hill where the park now stands. At Hospital Rock, 100 yards from the memorial, 17 wounded colonialists were slaughtered without mercy. Only 25 men escaped; according to folk history that was due to Wood's use of the Masonic distress signal, which the Tory Brant

recognized and respected. Presumably the other 125 men weren't Masons.

After the Revolution the settlers returned in force, full of enthusiasm for the richness of their new young nation. Pennsylvania was bursting with minerals, particularly coal and iron ore. The only problem was access in this rugged mountain region. Rivers were inadequately navigable. Canals were needed— hundreds of miles of them—if mining was to be made economically feasible. So, with typical American fervor, the canals were built. In 1827 the British consul in Philadelphia reported home that "canals are opening everywhere!" New York's Erie Canal was completed in November 1825. Then came the Lehigh, the Delaware and Hudson, the Susquehanna and Tidewater, the Conestoga, the Monongahela and that incredible network that eventually stretched from Philadelphia to Pittsburgh, over 300 tortuous miles to the west.

Equally impressive was the gravity railroad linking Carbondale and Honesdale over the high mountain ranges of Wayne County. This was one of a series of such railroads built in the mid-1800s to carry the anthracite coal mined in the Lackawanna Valley, in the West, to the Delaware and Hudson Canal in the east, where it was barged on to Kingston.

The principle was simple. The cars, full of coal, were hauled up a series of planes by a stationary steam engine and then were allowed to coast the downhill slopes by gravity. On level stretches they were drawn by horses or mules. In this way they rolled by the hundreds into the sturdy town of Honesdale, where the coal was transferred into barges waiting in the canal basin. The return trip, a longer haul of 23 miles as compared with the outward journey of 15 miles, was made on a less arduous "light track." It was a dangerous business—cables would snap and brakes would fail—but it worked.

There are some photographs and postcards of the process in the museum on the main street in Honesdale. You can't miss the place—there's a 13,600-pound block of anthracite near the main entrance, and an old steam tractor and switch engine in the back yard. The canal basin used to be just behind the museum. It's filled in now but part of the rail tracks and sorting bins still remain, layered with coal dust. Over at Hawley, an old mill town south on Route 6, is one of the old passenger cars used on the gravity railroad.

Just up the road from the Honesdale Museum there's a full-size replica of the *Stourbridge Lion,* the first steam locomotive to run in America (the original is in the Smithsonian Institution, Washington D.C.). This magnificent creature was imported from England and was given its first trial in Honesdale on August 8, 1829 by engineer Horatio Allen. He later wrote: "As I placed my hand on the handle I was undecided whether I should move slowly or with a fair degree of speed, but holding that the road would prove safe, and proposing, if we had to go down, to go handsomely and without any evidence of timidity, I started with considerable velocity." Later tests showed that the locomotive was too heavy for the tracks, so for many years the canal company used mulepower, rather than replace the line, and the *Lion* remained docilely in a shed.

Strangely enough, the engine was not the only import from Stourbridge. That English town was also a glassmaking center, and Christian Dorflinger is said to have used many ideas from the companies there when he established his glassworks at White Mills, just south of Honesdale, in the late 1860s. There are even tales of English glasscutters, at that time considered to be the finest in the world, being smuggled over to America in wine casks. Today original Dorflinger-cut crystal is almost worth its weight in gold, and there's a splendid array in the museum at Honesdale.

To travel the narrow mountain and valley roads of this lovely corner of Pennsylvania, start in the village of Bethany a few miles north of Honesdale—a pleasant contrast to the gritty valley towns. Following the steep approach, visitors will find themselves on a wide green dotted with large shade trees. At the topmost corner is a Presbyterian church (1836) influenced by Wren's London churches, and surrounding the green are a series of fine old homes, including the David Wilmot Mansion. At the time of my visit this Greek Revival structure, with a large pedimented porch supported by four Ionic columns, was being refurbished by its new owners, but it will not be open to the public. Although he occupied many important positions of power, David Wilmot is best remembered for his Wilmot Proviso, banning slavery in the "new territories," and his effort to attach it to important congressional bills. The furor caused by his actions led to the creation of the Free Soil Party, which later formed the basis for the Republican Party.

St. Tikhon Monastery—near South Canaan

Not far from the village is Bethany Colony, an unusual rural complex that includes The Mansion, with its seven dining rooms; a theater, formal gardens and recreational facilities; a motor inn, and private homes set in 500 acres of rolling meadows and woodlands. It's an interesting place to spend an evening or a weekend, particularly in the summer, when the theater is most active.

Farther south, past the old gravity railroad picnic grounds at Waymart, meander the lanes around South Canaan. On the road to Cortez I found an octagonal schoolhouse built of massive blocks of native stone and unused today. I only hope some local society is intending to ensure its preservation. It looked in need of repairs.

In the same area I was surprised to come across a series of Moscow-like onion domes thrusting their bulbous silhouettes over the trees. I stopped and strolled into the grounds of the St. Tikhon Monastery and Seminary, orginally established in 1905. Outside the church I met a man with a long black beard who invited me in. A service had just ended and the monks were leaving. The air was full of incense; candles gleamed and illuminated the richly painted icons and Baroque-style wood carvings that filled the interior. Not an inch of the walls and ceilings was undecorated. Flowers, vines, crosses, jewels, murals, madonnas, chandeliers, saints, banners, Bibles, gleaming lecterns—the place seemed like a golden storehouse of ancient treasures. The monks, in contrast, were dressed in rough black robes and sandals. My guide, who spoke with a thick Russian accent, explained that this was one of a number of Russian Orthodox establish-

ments in the region (the Scranton–Wilkes-Barre area contains a large number of Eastern European immigrants). He told me about his life as a monk, showed me the various buildings, including a delightful onion-domed belltower, and then invited me to join him and his brothers for dinner. Unfortunately I had made other arrangements and so declined his offer. I wish now that I had stayed. Most hidden-corners explorers would never miss an opportunity like that!

Travel eastward and follow the Lackawaxen River past beautiful Lake Wallenpaupack, through Kimbles and Rowlands. If you look carefully down by the river you will notice occasional segments of the old Delaware and Hudson Canal. Eventually you will return to the village of Lackawaxen, on the west side of the Delaware aqueduct bridge. This is one of my favorite spots. Below the rambling general store, with its old canal snubbing post, is the Zane Grey House, a little-known museum. This is where the creator of such western classics as *Riders of the Purple Sage* and *The Spirit of the Border* began his writing career, working on a battered lapboard. The place is full of Grey memorabilia. On the walls of his workroom are the oil paintings used as first-edition jacket covers, plus a generous selection of cowboy hats, leather breeches, original examples of Navajo art and a Morris chair, Grey's favorite working chair. Grey loved this place; he once wrote "My years in Lackawaxen represent more than a struggle to become independent through writing. Here I gained my first knowledge of really wild country and here I had my first happy times since early childhood." For all its history of Indian massacres, canal building, coal mining, gravity railroads and the like, the region remains tranquil—a lovely place in the Pennsylvania mountains to spend a few hours.

19. AN OUTDOOR COUNTRY MUSIC FESTIVAL

It is a hot September afternoon. The crowd is boisterous and beer-happy. An occasional whiff of marijuana floats across the fairground arena. Shirtless boys and girls in loose halters lie in piles around iceboxes. There are hundreds of young people in the field sloping down to the stage. Two massive walls of black loudspeakers face the audience from either side of the stage. The compère, a rather frail man in a wide-brimmed hat, is trying a few half-hearted jokes on the crowd as filler until the group has finished tuning its guitars, banjoes and fiddles.

Then there's that first booming chord—"A one, two, a one, two three, four"—and they're off—"Ladies and gentlemen, the Kutztown Good Time Arts and Music Fesitival is proud to present the Star-Spangled Washboard Band"—a great roar from the audience, followed by whistles, cheers, a few sailing beer cans—everyone's ready to dance—the music's just right.

Up they leap. Long hair, bead braids, loose shirts, bell-bottoms, all flapping. Dancing on rugs, raincoats, the grass, newspapers, even other people's stomachs. The music gets faster. It's crazy! It's over 90 degrees, and here in the middle of rolling hills and woods and grazing cows and slow, clear streams hundreds of people are prancing and dancing the afternoon away, as the band, sweating and smiling, pile on the pace, faster and faster and faster. How fast can you play "Orange-Blossom Special"? The banjo man's going crazy, the fiddle player has just about sawn his fiddle in half and the guitarist has lost at least two strings—and still it goes on—the crowd just goes on dancing and chanting—more, more, more, more, more—!

Music festival—Kutztown

20. COUDERSPORT TO NEW MILFORD

Journey Through the Endless Mountains

The region we'll explore is bounded on the north by the New York State line, on the south by Route 414, on the east by 81 and on the west by 44. Towns include Oleona, Azilum, Coudersport, Wellsboro, Athens, Montrose and New Milford.

There's something about northern Pennsylvania that attracted all manner of pioneers during the colonial days. Many groups settled in the lower plains south of the mountains, but others desired more isolated enclaves, safe from external influences, where their lifestyles could be pursued in a state of pastoral permanence. The "Endless Mountains" of Pennsylvania were a perfect environment. Particularly fascinating are two groups—a colony of Norwegians led by the famed concert violinist Ole Bull, and a group of aristocratic refugees from the French Revolution, who founded their community of Azilum in a secluded valley near Towanda, on the rugged northern edge of the state.

Let's begin with Ole Bull and the Norwegians. I set off in search of the site of their community from Williamsport on Route 220. The air was crisp as I drove north up Route 44 toward Coudersport. Soon the broad forested valley had narrowed to a rugged alpine ravine. The road twisted and turned, climbing higher into the hills, and the weather began to change. Fluffy white clouds were replaced by ominous groups of gray thunderheads. The larger forest trees on the lower slopes dwindled to a more sparse vegetation of stunted oaks, hemlocks and pines. The wind lashed the branches, and leaves, still green, were flung in scurries across the narrow two-lane road. Suddenly, following a sharp crack of thunder directly overhead, a rainstorm hit the mountain like a tidal wave. The road was transformed into a streambed. Water hurtled downhill, briefly pausing to gather in pools before continuing its descent. Trees bent low in the gale that tore across the ridges. Bits of bark flew past the window. The windshield wipers were useless, so I pulled onto a hard shoulder to sit out the storm.

As I slowly descended the narrow road into the Oleona Valley, the storm passed and the sun reemerged in a blue sky. White clouds returned and the ground was misty. It was like looking down into the heart of a volcano—the whole valley was glistening and steaming. Only as I dropped lower could I make out trees and fields. This might have been Norway, one of those high fjeld valleys above the fjords. Grieg would have recognized the scene. His powerfully languid music would express both the beauty and drama of the setting while reflecting the ultimate dominance and the great eternal rhythm of the elements.

It must have been a similar sight that attracted Ole Bull to this secluded part of the mountains. The date was 1852. Bull was enjoying a second tour of American concert halls, where he astounded audiences with his virtuosity and dramatic approach to violin playing. Gordon Bennett, in his New York *Herald,* proclaimed

Miniature stave church—near Carter Camp

him "The Prince of Violinists." Bull loved the adulation, as he loved the people, the sturdiness and freedom of the young America. In contrast, he hated what was happening in his own native Norway, where Swedish domination was stunt- ing cultural growth and expression. So, in his impetuous way, he decided to found a colony for poets, artists and writers of his native land in the mountains of northern Pennsylvania. No time was wasted, and in September 1852 he unfurled the "Oleona" banner from the top of a pine tree. Within a year more than 400 Norwegian settlers had moved in. Bull had a log castle erected on a high point overlooking the valley and spent rest periods here during his busy concert schedule. The colony seemed to be flourishing.

Then abruptly he found that he had been swindled by a land agent and did not own the 11,000 acres he had "purchased." Lawsuits followed, but all to no avail. The colonists were expelled (some say at gunpoint), and tales are told of the dreadful hardships they suffered as they moved westward to Wisconsin. Bull lost a fortune and left America in 1857. The colony that began with such high hopes had vanished. All that remains today is the foundations of Bull's castle, at Ole Bull Park on Route 144 to Renovo, and a fascinating little museum run by Inez Bull, a descendent of Ole Bull, on the road to Carter Camp.

I found the place by chance. There's a small sign and a miniature version of a Norwegian stave church just by the gate. Inez greets visitors at the door to her cottage and takes them on a guided tour of the "Doll's House" and the tiny church before leading them into the museum. Here, while guests munch on cook-

ies and sip soft drinks, Inez relates the story of Ole Bull and Oleona. She insists that Ole had a perfectly legal deed to the land and that it still belongs to the Bull family, although she doesn't intend to claim it because "I can't possibly afford to pay the back taxes to 1853." Inez herself, a concert pianist and singer, sponsors the Ole Bull Music Festival at Carnegie Hall in New York, and visitors are requested to donate to the festival fund. She's a fiery lady of character. The walls of her museum are covered with memorabilia—letters from Presidents; Bull's christening gown; old portraits of the violinist; handicrafts made by her mother, Lady Johan Randulf Bull, and old Carnegie Hall posters.

Much farther to the east, in a more gentle landscape near Towanda, are the restored remnants of the French colony Azilum. The late 1700s were a bad time for French aristocracy. The revolution had made residence in France impossible, and the slave uprising in Haiti (Santo Domingo) had destroyed the old colonial way of life. The gentry dispersed widely over the western world. One group was attracted by the offer of a refuge made by several Philadelphia entrepreneurs, and they founded their sturdy community on the banks of the Susquehanna about 10 miles east of Towanda (follow the markers). Some 50 log houses were constructed around a marketplace. There were also taverns, stores, a gristmill, a distillery—even a theater. Local settlers were impressed by the civilization of the place. The French introduced glass windows and wallpaper and even gave concerts and balls. They also erected a vast two-story, fifteen-room log structure, La Grande Maison, with 16 fireplaces and large French windows opening out onto the river garden. Some historians claim it was built specifically for Queen Marie Antoinette, who was guillotined in Paris before she had a chance to visit her new home. Loyal supporters struggled to keep the colony going. However, by 1803 many had decided to return to Paris, following Napoleon's amnesty, or to move south to Savannah or New Orleans. Those who remained were instrumental in founding nearby towns, and Azilum itself was abandoned. Today it is being reconstructed as a shrine to America's French heritage. There's even talk of rebuilding the log "palace," which was destroyed in the 1840s.

Although Oleona and Azilum are perhaps the best-known colonies in the Endless Mountains, there's another equally interesting settlement farther to the east, named after Horace Greeley, the irascible publisher of the New York *Tribune.* He founded the colony of Sylvania here in 1842, basing it upon such utopian socialist principles as common ownership of property and the equal division of labor. The community's strict covenants included a female ruler, which was regarded by many as a prelude to disaster. Disaster did in fact come a brief three years later, when Sylvania's self-sufficient economy collapsed after a crop failure, and most of the 400 colonists, many from wealthy New York families, moved on to less arduous environments. Today there's little left to suggest the unusual beginnings of the place. The descendents of the colonists who remained can still be found in the town of Greeley, which, like much of the region, is a popular summer resort.

The Endless Mountains are one of Pennsylvania's finest yet lesser-known resort areas. Route 6 from Coudersport to Tunkhannock can get a little hectic during the summer, but there are so many places to visit that hidden-corners explorers will quickly find their own favorite enclaves, undisturbed by tourist traffic.

Let's make the drive, beginning at Coudersport, an important commercial center when this northern sector of Pennsylvania was one of the chief timber resources in the eastern part of the country.

At Sweden Valley, just off Route 6, is the Coudersport Ice Mine. Visitors taking Route 44 through Oleona will approach it at the end of a long descent following an arduous and awesome drive along the old Coudersport–Jersey Shore Turnpike. Folktales of highway robberies and mountain brigands seem only too real here, especially on the unpaved sections beyond Carter Camp. But, if your car is sturdy, it's a drive that should not be missed.

The tiny ice mine grotto is one of those freaks of nature, bewildering to the non-scientist. In the side of the hill there's a vertical shaft about 400 feet deep. During the spring, as temperatures outside increase, huge, tapering icicles begin to form in the shaft. Some more than 3 feet thick and 25 feet long have been recorded. This process continues through the summer, but as winter approaches, ice formation ceases, the icicles disappear and the shaft remains dormant until the following spring. During July and August the sight of all that ice and the coolness of the "mine" are a most welcome relief.

A few miles farther east along Route 6 is the Pennsylvania Lumber Museum. In an excellent series of exhibits, including a reconstructed logging camp featuring a bunkhouse, mess hall, blacksmith shop and Shay locomotive, visitors can gain a thorough understanding of life in the lumber country. It was an arduous existence. The tools were crude, the hours long and the dangers great, particularly in the spring when the logs, felled and trimmed during the winter months, began their long journey downstream to the sawmills. Many of the lumberjacks preferred to avoid the "drives"—a man could die a grisly death if he made one wrong move on those rotating, rollercoasting logs. But the pay was good and the floating "ark" cookhouses that followed the drive made sure the men were well fed every night. And at the end of the drive it was carnival time. Williamsport, to the south, was one of the world's most important lumbering centers during the late nineteenth century. It was here that lumbermen poured in for their blasts at the end of the season. Whisky tumbled down a thousand dry throats faster than the Susquehanna roared through the town.

The valley drive between Coudersport and Wellsboro is magnificent, one of the most impressive scenic routes in eastern Pennsylvania. The culmination is of course the "Grand Canyon of Pennsylvania," west of Wellsboro. I came there for the first time one summer evening. It was unusually quiet. Most of the visitors had gone and there was no one at the lookout to disturb the silence that filled the forested ravines below. Way, way down, the silver band of the river swept around the bluffs, deep in shadow. Strolling away from the platform, with its wire fence and coin-in-the-slot telescopes, I sat on a rock between two pines, looking over the mountains and the endless forests that stretched to the horizon in all directions. There was the faintest swish of leaves and branches, almost like a lapping tide on a beach. Crickets chirped and an eagle spiraled high above the valley. There is a great peace here. It's a place to experience again the unity, the harmony, of all things. And it's a place many come back to—it stays in the mind a long time.

East of Wellsboro the scenery softens. The valleys are less dramatic and the countryside becomes more rolling. Beyond Troy, an interesting town with a splendid collection of Victorian mansions, there are scores of back roads meandering through the hills of Bradford County. At Luther Mills I found a lovely old covered bridge, and farther east in the country around Le Raysville and Rome I came across groups of Amish and Mennonites. It seems that this part of the state continues to attract pioneer people. Earlier ones have long gone, but these sturdy families are unlikely to leave. This area represents an extension of their Lancaster County base, and their appetite for farmland is insatiable!

The eastern section of the Endless Mountains is rich in museums. Montrose, eastward on Route 706, possesses two, and outside New Milford at the end of our journey there's a living museum in the form of Old Mill Village. The recent injection of state funds should provide the expansion necessary to make this outdoor exhibit truly representative of the architecture and lifestyles of northern Pennsylvania. A good start has been made; on summer weekends visitors pour in to watch craft demonstrations such as soap-making, thread spinning, cloth weaving, pottery, blacksmithing and rug braiding. It's an excellent spot to rest after that long, lovely drive through the Endless Mountains.

Covered bridge—Luther Mills

21. HAWK MOUNTAIN SANCTUARY

The sanctuary, established in 1934 as a model of wildlife conservation techniques, is best known for its fall flights of hawks and eagles.

It is located approximately 8 miles north of Hamburg, Pennsylvania (junction of Routes 61 and 78), and 18 miles east of Pottsville. The most scenic approach is from the east off Route 78, via Krumsville, Kempton and Eckville.

I first came here on an autumn afternoon. The sky was a brilliant blue. The sun was warm but the sear of summer was gone and the breezes were cool in the shady places. I climbed up the hill along the soft wood-chip path and strolled across the bridge to the north outlook. There was no one around; I had the mountain to myself. The only sound was a whispering of wind as it topped the crest. Leaves, barely flecked with scarlets and bronzes, rustled together comfortably.

I sat on a slab of white rock and looked eastward over the bowl of forest enclosed by the hills. A boulder-strewn stream tumbled through the trees and out into the rolling plain beyond. Tiny white farmhouses and barns nestled in a patchwork quilt of green fields disappearing on the far horizon in the faintest of hazes.

Soaring high above my platform, soaring up in spirals, were two golden eagles. Their wings, outstretched to their very limits, never moved. They circled together. Far below, their shadows moved across the treetops.

I watched a raccoon pick its way through the wild rhododendron bushes. It turned and looked up at the eagles. Its striped tail was erect and its front paws, humanlike in their delicate structure, were tensed, ready for rapid escape. But the eagles were oblivious to its presence. They were far too high to plunge and seemed to be thoroughly engrossed in their spiraling flight. The raccoon sniffed, scratched its ear with a daintily outstretched finger and moved into the shadows under the hemlocks and pines.

I was lucky. I had chosen a quiet weekday to come up here. Weekends during May and June, when the rhododendrons and laurel bloom, or October and November, when the migrations of eagles and hawks occur, tend to be a little crowded.

Make sure to visit the sanctuary headquarters. There's a small but interesting display here describing the migration patterns of North American birds, and a minisanctuary outside for smaller birds.

Country scenes—near Hawk Mountain

Also, explore the farmlands to the east of the mountains around Steinsville and Wanamakers. This is real Pennsylvania countryside, with huge red barns, old inns shaded by maples, crisp Victorian villas, moss-covered roofs and bowed fences. Follow the lanes at random, the bumpier the better. It's hard to lose your way. High above the undulating fields there's always the silhouette of Hawk Mountain, silent guardian of the valley.

22. HUNTINGDON TO LEWISBURG
The Kishacoquillas Amish

Here's a Pennsylvania region of quiet people, little-known state parks, old market towns and steep mountain drives. It is located between Williamsport and Harrisburg and bounded on the north by Route 45, on the south by 522, on the east by the Susquehanna River and on the west by Huntingdon on Route 22. Towns include Belleville, Reedsville, Northumberland and Lewisburg.

I was sitting by a cornfield in the Kishacoquillas Valley. It was one of those balmy summer evenings when everything pauses. No butterflies fluttered over the corn tassles, bees were dozing in their hives, leaves lay still, glistening with the juices of July. Nothing moved. I had just completed a splendid dinner of sautéed scallops and salad. The camper stove was working for a change and coffee was brewing. The aroma was wafted on the air, mingling with the sweet scents of evening, and I reclined in my folding chair enjoying a clean-drawing pipe.

I heard a faint clip-clopping sound in the distance, over the dip in the road. Then I saw a buggy, very square and black, emerge over the far rise, drawn by a brown pony. It disappeared briefly into another dip but the clip-clopping grew louder. Then it was in front of me and slowing. The man driving it wore a wide-brimmed straw hat, a white linen shirt crossed with prominent suspenders, brown trousers and sported a huge red beard. Over the same hill came a second buggy identical to the first. The driver wore exactly the same outfit and had an even larger beard, deep rust in color. I rose to speak. One of the horses shied nervously but the two gentlemen remained immobile, staring at me, my clothes and my camper van. I felt a little uncomfortable and made some inane comment about its being exceptional weather for the time of the year. There was no reply—just more staring. So I followed up with an elaboration on the point, saying how pleasant it was to be in a place as quiet as this, and did they live around here. Silence—utter and complete. I couldn't think of much else to say. I tried a weak smile. No response. I was just about to make another dumb remark when they flicked their reins in unison and clip-clopped off down the road and over the hill. I stood watching until they vanished behind a cornfield and felt rather unwelcome in this lovely valley.

"Oh, don't mind them Amish boys." I visited a store in a nearby village, filled with mounds of fresh fruit and vegetables, homemade jams and pickles, locally cured hams, bacon and shoulders, and large sacks of sugar and flour. Just the smell of the place would suffice for a meal. "No, they don't mean t'be offensive" the storeowner told me, "they jus' don't talk too much to strangers, y'know, they like t'keep to themselves."

"I didn't know this was Amish country," I said.

"Why, valley's full of 'em. They got all kinds of different names but they's all the same really—real proud of it too."

The Amish must have sensed the peace of the valley when they first began settling here around 1790. This was at a time when, driven by the constant need for more land (an Amish farmer is expected to provide each of his sons with a new farm), Amish and Mennonites together moved out of the now famous "Pennsylvania Dutch" country around Lancaster.

Isolation from external influences enabled the religious settlers to preserve their unique lifestyle. They celebrated their Sunday evening "singings" in the homes of the members of the faith. Churches at that time were considered superfluous. They dressed in simple, buttonless clothes, avoided mechanical devices of all kinds, rode in plain buggies drawn by horses, painted their homes white (although blue-painted gates were said to indicate the presence of a marriageable daughter in the family), unofficially condoned the custom of "bundling," made use of their own doctors, or "pow-wowers," and ate gigantic multiplatter meals which included such delicacies as "sweet-sours" (pickled vegetables), kalbsskopt (mock turtle soup), spanjerkel (stuffed and roasted suckling pig), hinkelpie (chicken pot pie), kalbsbraten (roast veal) and even kuttleflick (soused spiced tripe)—not to mention a vast array of cold meats, vegetables, apple butter, cracker pudding and pies.

The strictures of the lifestyle, however, were so well defined that the slightest variation gave rise to the threat of "shunning" (excommunication). Splinter groups developed rapidly, and today the valley is undoubtedly "the most divergent expression of Amish culture anywhere in North America." Hostetler in his *Amish Society* identifies 10 groups here, including the two ultraconservative "Nebraska" sects ("Nebraskas 1881" and "Nebraskas 1948") and the Byler Amish ("Bean Soupers"), moderate groups such as the Peachies and Zook (Speicher) Amish, and five more contemporary "Church Mennonite" groups, each of which has its own church and its own set of customs and norms.

The distinctions are infinitely subtle. The "old school" (Nebraska) Amish males do not wear suspenders, have shoulder-length hair, ride white-top buggies and do not paint their barns, whereas the slightly less conservative Bean Soupers ("old church") males have shorter hair, wear one suspender, ride yellow buggies and paint their barns. The Zooks go one step further. The men are allowed two suspenders, short hair, painted barns and such luxuries as carpets, electrical appliances and even "wall mottoes" in their homes. The more contemporary groups, as one might expect, place even less restriction on clothes and use of electrical equipment, although the Locust Grove Mennonites do have a taboo on sleeveless dresses and make-up for women. It all gets very confusing!

Yet for all the social fragmentation the valley possesses a distinct unity of beauty, silence and peace. Few vehicles travel the back roads and tracks that crisscross the farmlands (although on one occasion I was passed by a souped-up dune buggy with glass-flecked paintwork driven by some errant young Mennonite). Large, graceful barns stand at the side of diminutive white farmhouses. Names such as Stoltzfus, Zook, Beiler and Nolt appear often on roadside mailboxes. Of course the religious devotion of the inhabitants is occasionally evident. Road-

Coburn

side signs, in white lettering on a stark black background, bear such encouraging messages as "After Death—The Judgment." A poster in a Belleville store window reads: "All Night Singing—Featuring The Galileans, Blessed Praise, Gospel Harmony And The Ambassadors of Hope."

As you move westward, out of the valley toward the Susquehanna River, the roads between Lewistown and Lewisburg/Sunbury provide some of the finest driving in central Pennsylvania. The route from Lewistown via Reedsville, Port Ann and New Berlin is particularly recommended. It passes through or close to numerous state parks where, if you're on a relaxed schedule, you can choose between swimming, fishing, rock climbing, nature trailing or just plain lying in the sun in a setting of streams, pine trees and wide valley views.

Poe Valley Park, approached by the rough Siglerville Pike Road, is worth the journey in a sturdy car. The first time I made the attempt from the Victorian-flavored village of Coburn on the north side of the range, I found my camper badly in need of shock absorbers at the end of the journey. If you approach the park this way, take a look at Coburn—it contains some delightfully idiosyncratic architectural details.

I also enjoyed the Reeds Gap Park a few miles east of Reedsville. There's an excellent swimming pool here set in the midst of a pine forest and, although there are petty restrictions about diving even when the pool is unoccupied, it makes a refreshing pause on a hot summer afternoon. Farther to the west at the Greenwood Furnace State Park there's another excellent bathing area in a cold mountain lake just off Route 305.

Leave time to explore the Susquehanna towns of Northumberland and Lewisburg at the end of this long drive eastward from the Kishacoquillas Valley. Northumberland, with its long, tree-shaded green, has the sedate appearance of a pros-

perous market town. Other towns in the region, notably Mifflinburg, Centre Hall and Middleburg, all have a similar flavor. There's a comfortable juxtaposition of large mansions with slightly pompous civic buildings, austere churches and commercial streets of relatively harmonious appearance.

A short distance from Northumberland's green is the Joseph Priestley house, where the English philosopher-theologian-chemist lived from 1794 until his death in 1804. He was described by his friend Jefferson as "one of the few lives precious to mankind." Impressive words, but his contributions to mankind, which included the discovery of oxygen (and the invention of soda water following experiments in a brewery), were overshadowed by his unorthodox views. Such views, which included support for the American and French Revolutions, led to the destruction of his home and laboratory in 1791 by a mob in Birmingham, England. He soon emigrated to America and planned to settle with a colony of English refugees in Northumberland. Although the colony itself never materialized, he lived comfortably on the banks of the Susquehanna and continued his experiments and writing until his death. Today close to the house is an excellent little exhibit that provides an informative overview of his achievements.

Lewisburg, home of Bucknell University, is the market center for a flourishing farming region. The portion of the town near the bridge seems to have changed little since the early 1800s, and there's a heritage tour pamphlet available. Down the cool side streets architectural extravagances abound—cupolas, mansards, oriole windows, elaborate chimney pots and rare "lie on your stomach" windows in the architraves of Greek Revival homes. There's no lack of enthusiasm for renovation here. Just above Water Street, the owner of a large Victorian mansion has painted the whole structure in glorious canary yellow with white trimming, like a rather mature bridesmaid at some extravagent wedding. Occasionally, though, renovation has been carried too far. The Packwood House on Market Street (open to the public) is one of the last remaining three-story log houses in the country and was originally built as a riverside tavern. Unfortunately no logs are to be seen today except for the fencing around the garden. The building has been re-sided in those tasteless pseudowood sheets that have ruined the appearance of so many fine old buildings. The house tour is worth taking though.

Outside the town, one mile to the north, is the ornately Victorian Slifer House, now a museum and display piece. When I strolled through the rooms admiring the richness of the furnishings, the abundance of complex architectural detailing, I thought of the orthodox Amish in the Kishacoquillas Valley and of their aversion to such material trappings as carpets and curtains, even bathtubs, inside toilets and paint. Their preferences are a matter of choice, not necessity. The Amish are by no means poor—in fact they are buying farmland by the hundreds of acres around Selinsgrove and Middleburg to the south and Bradford County to the north (see "Coudersport to New Milford"). Yet even in the last quarter of the twentieth century, many choose to live an austere existence that has changed little over three centuries. It is interesting that such divergent lifestyles did and still do exist in such close proximity. It says much for the mutual tolerance and understanding of the peoples who make up this quiltcloth of a nation.

23. LEESBURG AND VICINITY
The Virginia Hunt Country

Ever wondered how the wealthy—the really wealthy—live? Well, come and explore this corner, with its vast estates, horse farms and secluded villages, and you'll get some idea.

The region is located west of Washington, D.C., and is bounded on the north by the Potomac River, on the south by Route 66, on the east by 659 and on the west by Harpers Ferry and the Appalachian ranges. Towns include Leesburg, Middleburg, Hillsboro, Lincoln and Waterford.

There are two ways to explore the Virginia hunt country of Loudoun County. The more popular way is the well-traveled Route 50, which enters the area out of Washington. Visitors make the almost obligatory pause at the famous Red Fox Inn at Middleburg before whisking past extravagant country estates defined by white fences and manicured pastures, where foals prance among carefully groomed patches of daisies. Then they follow the official itinerary of "sights." Oatlands, south of Leesburg, is an unusual mansion built by a great-grandson of Robert "King" Carter (see "Northern Neck") in Classical Revival style. The enormous portico with Corinthian capitals, added in 1827, exaggerates the structure's disjointed appearance, but the formal gardens are worthy of exploration.

Next comes Morven Park, just north of Leesburg, once home of a governor of Virginia, Westmoreland Davis. In addition to the gardens, nature trails, exquisite tapestries in the great hall and a confusing variety of "period" rooms, this is also home of the International Equestrian Institute and a carriage museum.

After lunch in Leesburg, travelers following this standard route should visit the Loudoun County Museum on Loudoun Street and take the well-marked do-it-yourself walking tour of the town. This is obviously hunt country—where else would one find the Hunting Pink Country Boutique, the Tally-Ho Theater and the Horsemaster Tack Shop.

Finally, assuming visitors have only a day for this excursion, a tour should be taken of the famous Manassas Battlefield, between Warrenton and Fairfax, where two major Civil War confrontations took place, in 1861 and 1862 respectively. After all this traveling a fine dinner is in order at one of the many overpriced but creditable restaurants on the western outskirts of Washington, D.C.

Now for the alternative. If you're not particularly enthusiastic about guided tours, elaborately furnished country mansions and large signposted battlefields, there's another way to explore this beautiful region. First avoid Route 50 if you can. Much of it is brash and artificial. The estates and horse farms fronting the busy highway are not the "real" estates. The famous family names linked with the hunt country—Mellon, Du Pont, Johnson, Mars (not to mention the 80 or so other millionaires in Loudoun and Fauquier counties)—tend to seek seclusion. Often their residences are situated well away from main roads down long avenues of shade trees. There are no signs, no giveaway mailboxes—just miles of white fencing and stone walling. At $30 a foot, it is apparent that fortunes have been spent on pasture and boundary delineation alone. Local residents seem to be proud and protective of their celebrities. Don't bother asking directions to Paul Mellon's estate, especially in a town like Middleburg. You'll be likely to get a rather blunt rejection. As one of the storeowners told me, "It's natural, I suppose. People are fascinated by wealth. They say Mr. Mellon is worth a billion. Well, many people want to see just what a billion looks like, but it wouldn't be right, would it, for him to be bothered all the time? They say he's a good man. Well, I say leave him be. Give him some peace and quiet." I agree. When I make my first million I'll want some peace and quiet too.

So, avoid Route 50 and enter if you can from the north via White's Ferry.This is a lovely spot, particularly on an early weekday morning (weekends can get hectic). Picnic tables are scattered under the trees along the banks of the Potomac, and just back up the road is a crumbling sandstone bridge over the Chesapeake and Ohio Canal. The first spade of earth was dug for this impressive piece of engineering on July 4, 1828, the same day that the cornerstone was laid for the Baltimore & Ohio Railroad. It was competition all the way between the two transportation links. Although the railroad tended to dominate, the canal was ultimately completed from Georgetown to Cumberland and served as an important coal shipping link from the western Maryland mines to the Washington area. Today, although there are restored sections at both ends, most of the canal is a dry ditch paralleled by the old towpath, now a long-distance footpath. I met a hiker just by the bridge at Whites Ferry. He was walking the complete length of the canal with a well-thumbed guidebook full of the most detailed route descriptions. "About another ten days I should be in Cumberland. Had to stop for a couple of days 'cause of my feet—solid blisters. They're OK now." So saying, he took a final look at the bridge, tucked the guidebook into a pocket in his backpack and continued his walk. He turned and waved once. I waved back and thankfully returned to a picnic bench to watch the ferry moving across the river.

The *General Jubal Early* is basically a raft powered by a small motor. Loose chains at either end are designed to prevent cars from rolling off. They didn't look very strong. Still, I thought, this is an ancient Maryland institution; therefore it must be safe. Nevertheless I watched quite a few crossings before I finally decided to take the camper across.

The other side is a different world. Gone are all vestiges of the outer Washington suburbs. There are rolling, open fields, some dotted with strange rock outcrops, thick clumps of woodland and dusty country lanes. It's these lanes that give the region much of its charm. If you have time, follow them at random. Most are numbered, but if you're worried about getting lost there are detailed maps available at the county offices in Leesburg. I spent a whole day roaming the back roads and enjoyed some of the finest driving in Virginia. At times it's like journeying through a Constable masterpiece. I saw stallions racing each other across clover pastures, white-spired churches peeping over treetops, a herd of cows being led

C & O Canal towpath—near Leesburg

home for milking by a boy and his dog. Shafts of orange sunset filtered through the dust of the lane. I found an old one-room schoolhouse (the Mountain Gap School) on a lane just off Route 15, about four miles south of Leesburg. Also in the same area, on Route 650, I located the famous Rokeby Mansion (1754), where important Federal papers, including the Declaration of Independence and the Constitution, were hidden when Washington was attacked and burned by the British in 1814. Then I meandered along Routes 611 and 690 through the heart of hunt country. I even saw a red fox, its bushy tail extended like a broom, running for cover across a field. There were no hunts, however—those occupy the fall and winter periods.

Somewhere near Purcellville I paused, left the car, climbed a fence and sat in a pasture overlooking the first hazy ridges of the Appalachian chain and the deep gap at Harpers Ferry. What a view! I have no idea how long I remained there, watching eagles slowly spiraling in warm air currents and the sun growing larger as it fell toward the mountains. The air was thick with evening perfumes. Below me were farms with tall silos and white fences. Everything seemed to be in limbo; even the cows in the field were motionless. There was a great stillness over the landscape. It was the pause before dusk, before night. I had forgotten there could be such peace.

The following day I continued my exploration. As with much of Virginia and West Virginia, the Civil War is still fresh in the minds of local residents. Almost everyone I spoke to had a tale to tell, not of great battles fought by famous generals but of smaller incidents, sometimes just as bloody, and usually unrecorded in history books. I was shown the tiny cemetery north of Leesburg where victims of the Battle of Balls Bluff are buried. Then in Waterford, farther to the west, I met a resident who told me of the confusions of loyalty in Loudoun. The county was split between the Union and the Confederacy. Waterford and Lovettsville declared for the Union and formed the Loudoun Rangers. In Waterford itself, just up the hill from the main street, the Baptish church is pockmarked with bullet holes from a skirmish on August 27, 1862, between the Virginia cavalry and local rangers. A number of victims are buried in the cemetery across the road, and the plaque on the church wall tells of brothers engaged on opposite sides.

One of the most notorious groups of Confederate "privateers" operating in the area were Mosby's Rangers, led by Colonel John S. Mosby. By all accounts they used extremely effective guerrilla tactics to harass Union forces. Northern generals made repeated attempts to eradicate them, but to no avail. Finally, desperate and frustrated, General Grant issued orders in 1864: "Send [a division of cavalry] through Loudoun to destroy and carry off the crops, animals, negroes and all men under 50 years of age capable of bearing arms. In this way you will get most of Mosby's men."

General Auger led 650 men on this vicious mission and reported: "I have made a scape-goat of him for the destruction of private rights. Now there is going to be an intense hatred of him in this valley, which is nearly a desert."

This is typical of much of Civil War history—cruel, vindictive and disastrous for innocent people. The raids had little impact on Mosby. His fame increased and by the end of the war his muster rolls contained the names of more than 4700 men. He was later appointed United States Consul at Hong Kong.

It is these lesser known incidents that bring about a true understanding of the Civil War, just as it is the lesser known towns and villages of a region that often reflect its true character. Visit the small communities of Lincoln (south of Purcellville), Hillsboro (home of the mother of the Wright brothers and a place having some excellent examples of stone architecture), Paeonian Springs (once a popular mineral water spa) and Aldie (east of Middleburg), the site of a Mosby skirmish. There's an old mill here, erected in 1807, which until recently was still in active operation.

My favorite village is Waterford, nestling in its narrow valley: compact and totally charming. It began as a Quaker settlement, and in 1734 a mill was established on the site of the present structure. The name of Milltown was changed to Waterford following the arrival of a persuasive Irish shoemaker, and between 1810 and 1820 the town expanded along the creek as an important supply center for immigrants moving across the Piedmont into the Shenandoah Valley. Today there's a wealth of architectural styles to be found in the village, including a number of board-and-mortar structures, similar to the Swedish homes and barns that once dotted the flat coastlands around Delaware Bay in the seventeenth century. The weavers' cottage, thought to have been built in 1734, is an excellent example of

Weavers Cottage (1734)—Waterford

the building technique, and in common with several other properties in the village is owned by the Waterford Foundation. Since 1944 there has been a popular crafts exhibition on the first full weekend in October. Sponsored by the foundation to raise funds for its preservation efforts, it is known as the Annual Home Tour and Crafts Exhibit and attracts thousands over the three-day period. Fortunately for hidden-corners explorers, the village retains its composure and tranquillity for the rest of the year. The residents are hardly typical country villagers though; many well-known authors live in the vicinity. In the course of an hour I had two intense conversations, the first with a bank president in jeans and sweatshirt, the second with a middle-aged professor of English. Topics ranged over the rise of the intellectual elite, witchcraft, the values of the younger generation and the demise of Europe. Unexpected and delightful!

Before moving on, pay a final visit to Leesburg. After all, it is the largest town in the region and obviously takes pride in its charm (which it definitely has) and its popularity (from which it definitely suffers). I was most impressed by the modern county office extension adjoining the beautiful courthouse (1894). It is one of those rare examples of a contemporary structure designed with sensitivity for its surroundings. There are a few details I would wish to change, but it was refreshing to see this degree of respect for a town with true character.

A short distance away from the main street is the livestock auction center—a raucous place when the bidding is in progress (Mondays from 1 P.M.), and even more interesting on the first Monday of the month, when the place becomes a vast country market. If you've ever had an urge to buy one of those salt-cured, pepper-coated hams, with thick gourmet mold and meat almost plum-colored, then this is the place, assuming you don't have the time to go to Smithfield (see "Smithfield and Vicinity").

Finally, when leaving the region try to use Route 7 from Leesburg. About 10 miles east of the town there's the sturdy Broad Run Bridge, one of several designed by Claude Crozet, formerly a captain in Napoleon's army. All you need is a photograph of horses and hounds with red-coated riders crossing the stone arches, and you have the complete picture of Virginia's beautiful hunt country.

24. A FLOUR MILL

This secluded old mill, just south of Grottoes in the Shenandoah Valley, is one of the last such establishments operating in Virginia. It would also appear to be the birthplace of George Caleb Bingham, the Missouri artist whose famous works Jolly Flatboatmen *and* Canvassing for a Vote *are still popular today.*

The mill was purchased by Ira Colby in 1908 and is run today by his two sons, Ira and R. D. ("Dunc") Colby. Although there are no signs or markers indicating the hidden riverside location of the mill, the Colby brothers welcome strangers and will gladly provide a short tour of its somewhat complex multilevel interior if there's not much grinding going on. (Also ask for the Colby flour recipe pamphlet.)

Bags of plain self-rising flour are piled near the door. Note the Jersey Lily trademark—said to have been coined by a previous owner who was infatuated with the famous Lily Langtry (born on the Isle of Jersey in the English Channel).

There's only one problem here. Ira and "Dunc" are no longer young men, and they wonder who will carry on the grinding when they retire. Any takers?

Flour mill—near Grottoes

25. WARM SPRINGS AND VICINITY
Springs, Spas and Spelunking

For a beautiful off-season weekend around the Blue Ridge Mountains, follow this route through old spa towns and into the real Appalachian back country of Virginia.

The region, located east of Staunton, is bounded by 33 in the north, 64 to the south, 81 to the east and the West Virginia Line to the west. Towns include Hot Springs, Warm Springs, Sugar Grove and Dayton.

I had just spent a night at Skyland, the beautiful hotel on the Blue Ridge Skyline Drive. During the summer the place is packed, unpleasantly so. But in mid-September it's quiet. There were no crowds queuing for dinner at the restaurant and I spent a delightful hour after the meal, listening to songs and tales by a resident folk-singer.

The following morning I was up early and dropped through the ridge mists into the Shenandoah Valley. I had noticed a group of spring and spa towns on the map, west of Staunton and Lexington. Nobody could tell me much about them so

I decided to go and explore the area for myself and see if any of the old "healing" springs were still operating. The journey was fascinating. I found a region rich in history, charm and interest. It's one of my favorite spots in this part of the Appalachian chain.

I began at the hub of the region, at "The Hot" on Route 220 above Covington. Hot Springs is the best preserved and most famous of all Virginia's spa towns. It has the flavor of an alpine resort in Austria. The grandiose hotel, The Homestead, rises castle-like above the narrow winding streets. Exclusive apparel and gift shops abound. Large limousines purr in shrub-screened parking lots. Chauffeurs chat quietly together while their employers enjoy an early morning round of golf. Private planes and helicopters bring distinguished guests to the mountain top airfield. Young couples, doe-eyed and tweed-clad, stroll along Lovers Lane above the town and groomed mares canter between the huge oaks and elms, scattered over the 17,000 acre Homestead estate. It's a little world all to itself. The hotel provides everything a lady and gentleman of means might desire. For the more active there are three 18-hole courses, miles and miles of hiking trails, an olympic size skating rink, tenpin and lawn bowling, tennis courts, stables, ski facilities, trout fishing, indoor and outdoor pools and skeet and trap facilities. For those seeking more restful pursuits there are fringe-topped surrey rides, a sand "beach" surrounded by a high wall and authentically equipped with beach chairs and parasols, daily concerts, dancing, card rooms and, of course, the spa itself with a full range of mineral baths, saunas, whirlpools, massage rooms and gym. The methods used, claims the hotel literature, "embody the best practices of the older European spas" and include such odd sounding treatments as Salt Glo, Scotch Douche, Tub, Spout, and Hot Pack.

Hot Springs, quite frankly, is not to everyone's taste or pocketbook. I briefly enjoyed its comforts as a respite from back road campsites, but was happy to be on the move again.

My next stop was Warm Springs, a few miles up the valley. Here is an authentic-looking spa with two enclosed bathing pools, one for men and the other for women. There was a slight nip in the air when I arrived, and strolling across to the drinking spring, I saw steam rising off the stream that ran down the lawn. I dipped my hand in and found it was warm, gloriously warm. To be precise it was 98°, compared to the waters at Hot Springs that emerge at a temperature of 106°. Geologists believe that the heat is somehow connected with subterranean volcanic intrusions of high conductivity rock. Heat from deep in the earth is transmitted up these igneous fingers and any spring or stream that comes into contact with them is automatically warmed before it emerges from the earth. There are conflicting explanations but this seems to be most readily acceptable.

Both bath houses, old circular wooden structures painted white inside and outside, contain changing rooms and pools, slightly blue in color. What a delicious experience, to submerge oneself in this water and drift in a warm, womb-like cocoon. In former times, bathers used to remain in the water sometimes for hours, their bodies supposedly absorbing all those rich minerals and losing all rheumatic and arthritic ailments. Waiters would float mint juleps on little cork trays to them and some of the more dedicated among them would even drink the unpleasantly flavored spring water and convince themselves and each other that their health was improving by the minute. It was an unusual yet thoroughly respected ritual. The cream of society wended its way from the cities of the Piedmont and coastal plains up into the mountains beyond Lexington. Those coming from the south would make the "spa circuit " beginning at Hot Springs and wend their way slowly, pausing for weeks at a time, through the other watering places—Healing Springs, Warm Springs, Millboro Springs and Wallawhatoola Springs. There were variations in route and itinerary. White Sulphur Springs, Red Sulphur Springs, Minnehaha Springs, and Sweet Springs, all just over the border in West Virginia, were equally popular resorts. Each claimed unique variations of water-content and restorative properties.

The rituals were precise and exacting. At White Sulphur Springs, particularly popular with the elegant plantation society of the Old South, separate rows of resort cottages were built, each with its own social classification. Paradise Row was for the newlyweds and eager debutantes whereas adjoining Wolf Row contained the young bloods, the dashing bachelors, all carefully screened and scrutinized by match-making matrons.

A writer who used the nom de plume Peregrine Prolix satirically exposed much of the myth concerning the properties of mineral waters which he suggested contained: "a very strong infusion of fashion [which is] gradually increasing, and no

doubt contributes greatly to the efficiency of the water." But thousands of health seekers ignored these teasing pieces and continued to pour into the mountain communities every year claiming cures for all manner of unusual ailments. Again Prolix had his own opinions and among his list of restorative capabilities he included the diseases of: "Black Plague, Blue Devils, Hydrothorax, hydrophobia, hypochondria, hypocrisy, diarrhea, die-of-anything, gormandising and grogging and all bad habits except chewing, smoking, spitting and swearing."

The Civil War brought the spa era to a close. Southern society particularly was decimated and wealth-consuming summers in the mountains no longer seemed relevant during the rigorous reconstruction era. A few centers like "The Hot", "The Warm" and "The White" have remained but many resort towns just closed up and died within a few years. Little remains of them today except unusual names on old maps.

Fortunately though, springs and spas are not the only features of interest in the region. In Warm Springs just down the road near the courthouse is Gristmill Square, a tiny collection of craftshops and a restaurant in a restored riverside mill. The project has been sensitively designed, especially the tiny Simon Kenton Pub inside the Waterwheel Restaurant where many of the shafts and fixtures of the old flour mill have been retained. Also a short walk from the square is the Bath County Historical Society open Friday and Saturday during the summer.

Nearby, a few miles west on 39, is the village of Bacova. Originally founded by

the Tidewater Oil Company as a lumber saw mill center in the 1920s, it was abandoned within a decade. Not until the 1960s did the town regain life when many of its homes were renovated and the old commissary building was converted into a crafts center and gift shop known as The Bacova Guild.

Avoid the main roads wherever you can in this region. Take the valley back roads towards and beyond Monterey and Sugar Grove. This is the real Appalachia. Much of the land is still thickly forested. Fresh streams tumble off hillsides and plunge into deep pools, shaded by trees and ferns. This is not warm water territory. Some of the pools are ice cold even in the midst of summer but if you can stand the first ten seconds of shock, a swim is one of the most luxurious of experiences on a hot afternoon.

Notice the architecture as you drive northwards along these silent valleys. Much of it is original log construction with tiny windows, thick shingled roofs and huge hinged doors. It's sometimes hard to distinguish houses from barns. They're all built to the same basic pattern—sturdy, rigid and dependable. The Sugar Grove area, just over the border in West Virginia, contains some excellent examples. Try to get up close to one and study its construction. The apparent simplicity of the design disguises a score of subtle details all developed to increase its durability. The people and the buildings are somehow alike. The men have brown grained faces like wood bark, and eyes black as knotholes. They walk straight but slow. They don't waste time in trivialities including pointless conversation. Many may not respond to idle questions from tourists. How-

Back country scene—near Monterey

ever if you're in trouble and need help, you'll get it without fuss. Some call them hillbillies. They don't seem to mind. It's a term that recognizes their separateness. If they detect any derision however, especially from outsiders, they're not beyond grabbing a shot-gun from the walls and blasting a load of buck shot at a fleeing backside. They hate interference. They avoid social workers, researchers and other " 'quisitive bodies" as much as possible. They believe that each family must solve its own problems independently. That's what life means to them—accepting and dealing with their own problems without outside help. They know things are changing. They know they will more than likely lose their sons or grandsons "to the world." But they stubbornly fight that day when their way of life will be gone. They fight it with everything they've got.

Equally independent in spirit but somewhat more sophisticated in manners are the Old Order Mennonites, centered around Dayton, near Harrisonburg. They also resist outside interference in their affairs but have ensured their continuity far better than the mountain people, by developing a solid economic base and a livelihood attractive to future generations of the same family. The Mennonite order is not diminishing. If anything it is expanding as more and more farmland is acquired.

On the backroads around Dayton are the familiar horse and buggy warning signs near intersections. Sometimes the center of Harrisonburg is full of these little black carriages. Men in long beards and women in delicate bonnets stroll among more contemporarily dressed crowds. Mennonite or "Dutch" stores offer a marvelous range of local produce—homemade lye soap, buckwheat groats, custom-blended granola, brown rice, steelcut oats, brewers yeast and toasted wheat germ. In one of these stores in Dayton, an elderly lady in a bonnet with one of the happiest faces I have ever seen, led me, mother-like, around the shelves describing the different processed grains and their uses. We'd return every minute or so to the counter where she would give me thin slivers of locally produced cheeses and then set off again to another part of the store. We ended by swapping recipes and I left, having purchased pounds of delicious cheese. My favorite is the Swiss-type, a mellowed-cream color with tiny round holes and a sweet, rich aroma. The problem is, my cat enjoys it as much as I do, so I have to sneak pieces when he's not watching.

The region is full of things to do and places to visit. A few miles west of Harrisonburg is the Natural Chimneys Regional Park, a series of independent limestone columns, some 120 feet high, carved in this fashion by the Shenandoah River. From a distance the grouping resembles a medieval castle and, as if to complete the impression, jousting tournaments are held here on the third Saturday of every August. Many of the parks have bathing areas. The Chimneys Park boasts an olympic-size pool and over the stiff mountain climb to Brandywine from Harrisonburg there's a beautiful mountain lake adjoining the campsite in the Brandywine Park.

This is a popular area with spelunkers (cave explorers); caves are abundant in the valley near Front Royal (Skyline Caverns), New Market (Endless and Shenandoah), Luray (Luray) and Grottoes (Grand). Also south of Woodrow Wilson's birthplace at Staunton is a humpback covered bridge built in 1835. It spans the Dunlop Creek, west of Covington and the unusual design and length makes this one of the most remarkable structures in this part of Virginia.

If you happen to travel through this region in the fall, take one of the "foliage tours" organized from Monterey, capital of Highland County (west from Staunton). This little corner of the state is especially beautiful during the October season and if the Bicentennial celebrations were any indication, Monterey may become a center for fall festivals. The county is already well-known for its Maple Festival. Much of the locally produced syrup is shipped north to New England and packaged as the Vermont version!

What an area this is—springs, spas, fancy hotels, real backwood routes, lakes, caves and fresh maple syrup. Top all this with a night on the Skyline Drive, off-season, and you have an itinerary for a perfect vacation.

Country store—near Bland

26. ABINGDON AND VICINITY
The Mountain Empire

Although this is one of the most beautiful and secluded mountain regions in southern Virginia, there's still plenty here for the active traveler—theatres, state parks, museums, railroad rides and a coal mine open to the public.

The region, located north of Bristol, is bounded to the north by the Kentucky Line, to the south by 81, to the east by 77 and to the west by 23. Towns include Bland, Saltville, Abingdon, Big Stone Gap and Norton.

"Yep, kin ah he'p ye?"

An old man, brown and wrinkled like an autumn leaf rose slowly from a bench near the potbellied stove. Outside the lopsided country store, the wind howled through branches and gray clouds scudded across the mountain tops on the other side of the valley. I could just see the river between a paint splattered refrigerator and the pile of empty boxes, partially blocking the store window.

There were three other old men sitting on the benches around the stove. The heat was welcome. Outside there was a sting of winter in the fall wind. They all turned from the television, precariously placed on a sagging shelf, to watch as I selected some snacks for lunch. There was little fresh produce and the shelves were sparsely filled. A low-watt bulb flickered above the counter. Business was decidedly slow in this small country emporium.

Conversation lagged. The old men all knew one another. They had debated, discussed and disagreed on every subject dear to their hearts and a few others besides. There was no need to talk. There was no need to go anywhere and there was no need to do anything but half-watch television, doze in the warmth of the stove and gaze at the occasional stranger.

The few buildings at the crossroads were old and roughly painted. A large oak creaked in the wind and a fluster of yellowed leaves flew from a branch and scurried down the road to the river. A woman in a dark shawl put out a cat and closed the door tightly behind it. The cat sniffed the breeze, ruffled its fur and reluctantly moved down the path, disappearing behind a bush. There was no traffic. It was a typical fall afternoon in this crossroads community without a name.

Down the road, a hundred yards or so, the valley widened. Long broad vistas of the Appalachian mountains stretched south-westwards in a curve. Below the primary ranges, uniform in height and profile, smaller hills clustered together away from the river. They were sharp-edged and steep sided. Narrow canyons wriggled between them. There were tracks up to the entrances but they disappeared in a jumble of dense vegetation and dark shadows.

"Sure, 'es some folks live up 'ere. Don' see t'much of 'em mind. Only comes down in the valleys once in a while f' food n' stuff."

I had paused to chat with one of the villagers on his way to join the others around the stove in the store. "Some of 'em grows 'baccy an' a bit o' corn. But its po' land in them hollers. Lord knows how they make a living. Wouldn't never ask 'em. Testy bunch o' critters. Let 'em be, tha's what I say, jes let 'em be. If they wan'a live up there, let 'em, I say. Me, I like it down 'ere. Bit more company."

I had left Route 77 at Bland, north of Wytheville, and immediately entered another world. Behind me were the superhighways and the sophisticated cities. I found myself driving south-westwards on Route 42, following the gentle sweep of the mountains, and the undulations of a silent valley. There are few settlements along the beautiful backroads in this area—an occasional huddle of buildings at a crossroads but for the most part there are just roadside farms. Between Abingdon and Gate City is part of the Burley tobacco belt. The curing barns are very different from those found around South Boston and Kenbridge (see Danville and vicinity). Farmers there use the flue-curing method that requires tightly sealed sheds, tall and windowless. The sheds in the Abingdon area are broader at the base and not as tall. The tobacco is "air-cured" and the barns are equipped with abundant doors, vents and hinged flaps to ensure adequate flow-through of air. The process is a slow one, far slower than flue-curing, but the resultant tobacco is highly prized by pipe smokers and snuff takers.

The pace of life reflects the slow pace of tobacco curing. At the time I was there, I saw little sign of activity anywhere in the valley. The harvest was in. All the scores of tedious tasks that go into the production of a sound tobacco crop had been completed. The migrant workers who had flocked into the valley for the cutting, had left. The tenant families living in ramshackle sheds often hidden from the road behind trees or lost in the hollows, were resting. The farmers, beyond a daily inspection of the curing sheds, had little to do. Some of them would join the " ole folk" up at the store for a chat. Others would just hang around at home, thinking of the upcoming auction when a year's work would be assessed, graded, and sold off to the highest bidder within a few seconds (see "Danville and Vicinity").

Saltville is the only town of any size between Bland and Gate City. The setting is magnificent, at the confluence of five valley roads and surrounded on all sides by sweeping mountain ranges. Just west of the town there's a swampy basin full of brackish pools and thin marsh grass. Old wood stumps and bits of machinery, cog wheels and iron beams, peer out of the water. It's a silent, somewhat eerie place, particularly in the early morning when stunted trees without leaves rise like dark phantoms and seem to writhe as clammy mists eddy across the water.

Once this abandoned waste was a vigorous salt mining center, hence the name of the town. During the Civil War, when salt was essential for preserving meats and other food supplies for the army, the community was known as "the salt capital of the Confederacy." Numerous skirmishes took place in the area, the most

bloody being the "Saltville Massacre" in the Broady Bottom–Church Ridge area. Earthworks and trenches can still be found in the hills surrounding the town and the conflict is regarded by many as the worst atrocity of the Civil War.

Salt making began here in 1788 and was expanded considerably in 1799 by William King who sank a 200 foot shaft to reach the brine. Today a small park, on the western edge of town, above the swamp, commemorates the shaft and provides a small permanent exhibition of the salt making process. Under a wide roof are a number of the "old method" cast iron kettles, each of which holds 100 gallons of brine. Fires are lit in the brick ovens beneath the kettles and the water evaporates to leave the white crystals behind. During the summer there are demonstrations of this form of salt making and souvenir packages are for sale. Nearby is an excellent reproduction of a log cabin, which illustrates a once familiar construction method in the region. In Saltville itself, there are a number of such structures still standing including the Madame Russell House, and the King-Stuart House, originally home of William King, the salt mining entrepreneur and later, the residence of Mrs. Flora Stuart wife of 'Jeb' Stuart, the Confederate cavalry general. The house is located close to Salt Park and is normally open to the public.

Saltville is not particularly attractive although redevelopment in the form of the diminutive Saltville Museum has brought new interest and life to the center of town. Two steam locomotives built in the 1890s and used by local industries stand in the square. Also the nearby Salt Kettle Theatre presents over 60 performances by local talent during the summer months.

If you're a theater-lover, the place to go is the Barter Theatre at Abingdon, a few miles to the southwest. This unique institution was founded during the Great Depression, by Robert Porterfield, a boyhood resident of Saltville. He was an actor, out on his luck, in New York. The Shakespearean troupe with whom he had been performing had broken up. One evening, hungry and struggling to make ends meet as an elevator operator, he had a brainwave. Ham for Hamlet! Why not set up a theatre out in the country where no theatres existed and offer seats to local farmers and their families in exchange for food and produce. "We can eat the box office" claimed Porterfield and very soon he and a band of faithful followers set about establishing Abingdon's "Barter Theatre". After an initial period of uncertainty, the idea caught on. The box office was transformed at each performance into a cornucopia of food—jams, home-cured hams, bacon, fruit, butter, country sausages, eggs, honey—even tight bundles of tobacco and the occasional disgruntled cockerel were offered in exchange for seats in the stalls. The theatre soon gained a reputation far beyond its rural hinterland.

Today visitors to the theatre can still barter for entrance but are expected to bring produce worth approximately $2.50 a seat. The Playhouse, the Barter's experimental division across the street from the main theatre, also encourages the system. So if you have a summer evening with nothing to do and some home-made jams to spare, enjoy some high-quality theatre in Abingdon. Allow time, too, for exploring the town itself. It's a graceful community, full of Georgian and Federal-styled residences many of which have been converted into attractive stores and craft shops. The famous Martha Washington Inn, set in a twelve-acre park, is a particularly delightful place to spend a day or two. All the rooms are furnished in original antiques and the dining room features real southern cooking including of course, country cured ham, fried chicken, spoon bread and hot biscuits. Unfortunately the barter system is not recognized here.

To the northeast of Abingdon near Marion is the Hungry Mother State Park, a popular recreation area complete with lake and beach, all at 3500 feet in the midst of the mountains. To the north beyond Richlands is the Breaks Interstate Park, "Grand Canyon of the South," where the Russell Fork River has carved out a canyon more than 1600 feet deep and at one particular point loops around a gigantic rock precipice known as The Towers. Although the canyon "has clothes on" for most of the year, the dense woods tumbling down the mountain slopes to the churning river below only serve to heighten the drama and the wilderness.

To the south of Route 81 near Marion and Bristol is the extensive Mount Rogers National Recreation Area, part of the Jefferson National Forest. Take time to drive the backroads through these ancient forests or follow the hiking trails up White Top and Mount Rogers (5729 feet). This is Appalachia as it was—untamed streams and waterfalls, open rolling hills, deep shadowy glades among the pines, cascades of rhododendron blooms, abundant wildlife, including the occasional bear and mountain lion. There are broad vistas of mountain-ringed valleys, hillsides blazing in scarlets and golds during the fall season, views of five states from the tops of the ridges.

To the southwest near Gate City is a major attraction, the Natural Tunnel State Park. This huge rock arch is said to be the remains of a large cave formed during the Pleistocene Age. The ceiling is more than 100 feet high and the width an average of 150 feet. It's an awesome place. There's a railway line through the tunnel and it can be a most alarming experience to meet an oncoming train while walking along the narrow footpath. The brochure claims there's plenty of room for both and advises "don't panic". The writer obviously lacked first hand experience.

This whole region is full of the mystery and romance of the early frontier. Daniel Boone passed close by the tunnel in 1769 to explore the territory now known as Kentucky. Staunch pioneers of Scots-Irish settled in thickly forested valleys and hollows—and lived harshly independent lives. Families were clan-like in their closeness. Outsiders were not welcome.

Any semblance of meddling by government officials was discouraged if necessary by force. Feuding between clans was common. The famous Hatfield-McCoy vendetta was typical of relations between the hillbillies of Virginia, West Virginia, Kentucky and Tennessee. John Fox Jr's "The Trail of the Lonesome Pine" is considered to be an accurate portrayal of life during those violent times. It tells the tale of the love between a Virginia mountain girl and a young mining engineer from the East, sent to gauge the region's coal and mineral resources. It's a true story of progress versus stability—the feuding Tolliver clan trying to hold onto

Hungry Mother State Park

its heritage, the burgeoning young America encroaching upon the wilderness. Earl Hobson Smith adapted Fox's novel into an outdoor play, presented during July and August at the Playhouse in Big Stone Gap, next door to the house where June Tolliver lived while attending school in the town and a few miles up the road from the Natural Tunnel State Park. The story of Tolliver's "final acceptance of their inevitable destiny" is told against a background of regional folk music. The ending is happy, I suppose. In reality though it was often a disaster for many mountain people. The callousness, greed and downright dishonesty of the coal companies is still resented today by descendants of the clans. They sold their lands for a pittance, signed contracts they couldn't read and when they turned to other means for making a living such as whisky distilling, were hounded by the police. However, even today, the spark of independence still flickers. Mountain dwellers continue to oppose big new schemes for strip mining and the occasional illicit still is discovered by law enforcement officials. A recent report in the Bristol *Herald Courier* stated "a resident of Jewell Ridge was charged yesterday with possession of illegal whisky after Tazewell County sheriff's deputy and an Alcoholic Beverages Control Board agent raided and destroyed a 50-gallon still near his home." There's life in the hills yet!

If you travel north into the coal country around Appalachia, Norton, St. Paul, Richlands and Bluefield you'll see what happened in these beautiful hills and hollows as a result of "progress." This is real mining territory. This is where Red Poore and his followers tried to unionize to combat the strangle-hold of company

Coal mine—near Norton

scrip wages, company stores, company houses and company cemetries where worn out, black-lunged miners had their first and only rest. The words of the folk song that goes: " . . . one day older and deeper in debt, . . . I owe my soul to the company store," are understood only too plainly in the coal dust stained hollows. This is Harlan County country where in the '30s violence and murder was a hundred times more prevalent than in New York city. This is John L. Lewis territory. The "Battle of Evarts" in which many miners were killed was fought not far away in May 1931. "Gun thugs" hired by the companies used to discourage union activities, by murder if necessary. Companies would blacklist union miners and throw them out of the company homes. Even the unions themselves became repressive. As a local miner said: "The Czars of Russia could have learned something about tyranny from the leadership of the United Mine Workers." Appalachia of course, or specifically, the coal section of the Mountain Empire, received abundant attention during the Kennedy-Johnson era. Today many claim there have been improvements. Others are not so certain. A local newspaper editor said recently: "Scores of millions have been spent and I can't tell you a single solitary thing that has been accomplished."

An elderly gentleman, one of the curators at the interesting Pocahontas Village and Exhibition Mine near Bluefield, was more optimistic when I talked with him: "Why compared to how it was when I was young, it's real cozy up 'ere now. They're allus grumbling but they don't know how it was, they got no idea."

Many of the new-rich at Richlands would agree. There's fresh money in the hills and a few astute good ole boys have found it. These "rich hillbillies" live in luxurious ranch homes away from the mines. From their point of view, the great renaissance of Appalachia has begun.

Tourists rarely venture up in to the tiny hollow towns. Mining communities such as Stonega, Derby, Pardee, Dante, Castlewood, Cleveland are often missing from the road maps. But they're there alright. If you look, you'll find them (see "An Appalachian Coal Town").

Most visitors prefer the pastoral valleys further to the south. After visiting Natural Tunnel and other fine recreational areas, many go on to the Southwest Virginia Museum at Big Stone Gap or take a ride on one of the scenic railroads that abound in the area. There's the Rimrock, operating between Big Stone Gap and Norton, and occasional excursions on the Clinchfield from Erwin (Tennessee), and the Southwest Virginia at Hiltons, near Bristol. This last railroad provides a superb 2 hour, 22 mile trip and often features live folk music at the picnic area. It's a great way to spend an afternoon in this lovely part of Virginia.

27. AN APPALACHIAN COAL TOWN

The region looks tired. The towns, drained of their youngsters, drained of new capital, stand crammed in river valleys, gaunt like ghosts. Funeral parlors are squeezed in between empty banks and old drug stores. People's faces are gray; lines and creases are etched in coal dust. Mists swirl in the mountains surrounding the town. Their slopes slip steeply into tiny back gardens. After rain, streams of light brown mud run between houses and into the main street. Trucks splash through, spraying cars.

The pithead is further up the valley. You can't see it from Main Street. Occasionally smoke will drift in and if the wind's blowing east, you can hear the thud and clatter of the belts and the sorters.

This is coal country—a place apart—a hard place to understand. Experts by the score have written words by the million. Laws and Commissions and programs and handouts and emergency funds and disaster reliefs and more laws have come and gone, and it's still much the same. The company houses still stand. They're not owned by the companies any more, but they remain all the same. The "improved" places with new paint and inside toilets are lower down the hollows. The whites live here. Further up, close to the mine buildings are the older places. Mostly blacks live here. "Segregation?" I ask a foreman up near the shaft. "Not on your life," he tells me. "Just the law of economics. Them that has, has. Them that hasn't, jes' keep on gettin' screwed."

They say things are getting better. A miner can earn up to $70 a day—even more. Problem is there aren't so many jobs. For every miner earning good money there are three others sitting at home in those steep valleys listening to the crunch of machinery and the coal trucks crashing down the narrow mountain roads. If things are getting better there's not much sign of it yet.

28. DANVILLE AND VICINITY
The Bright-Tobacco Belt

Here's a fascinating journey through the southern Virginia countryside—the heart of tobacco country. We'll travel across the rolling Piedmont, visit small farms and old plantations, attend a tobacco auction and admire the great mansions, once the home of wealthy tobacco farmers.

The region, located east of Danville, is bounded to the north by 460, to the south by the North Carolina Line, to the east by 85 and to the west by 29. Towns include Halifax, South Boston, Kenbridge and Charlotte Court House.

"Awwwlright now . . . what'llyougivemeforthisone I gotfifteen sixteenalrightI got seventeeneighteen,nineteenandIgot twent', twent', twent'awwwlrightnowtwent' heyIgottwent'onetwent'two. . ."

The auctioneer's high-pitched monotone echoes through the vast warehouse. It's nine in the morning and the tobacco auction's just beginning at Neal's Warehouse in Danville. The auctioneer, an old looking young man in a toupee is walking backwards down a long row of tobacco "baskets". His eyes take on a glazed appearance when he begins his rhythmic, rapid chant. At his side is the warehouseman, flapping his hands, grunting, casting wary glances at the bid-

Tobacco auction—Danville

ders. He seems by far the most agressive of the group. He initiates the sale of each basket by shouting out the base price and the auctioneer takes over, watching the straggling line of bidders for telltale signs of bids—winks, nods, curled fingers, clenched fists and a rather unusual elbow twitch resembling an irate plucked chicken. The bidders are very calm, shuffling slowly up the rows, abstractly fingering, lifting and fondling samples from each of the piles of loose tobacco. They read the grading mark left by the federal inspector and begin their silent rituals. They are all experts. They all know everything there is to know about tobacco. They represent the big companies—Imperial, Lorillard, Reynolds, American, Liggett & Myers and the others. Many have done this for years. They can read the grade marks like newsprint. They know a pencil scrawled B4 FR on the sheet left by the grader means fair quality leaf tobacco with an orange-red tint as opposed to H 3L which would indicate a good quality smoking leaf tobacco of lemon color. It often takes less than 5 seconds for each 250 lb (maximum) basket to be sold to the highest bidder. Sometimes the pace quickens and the poor auctioneer, who is obliged to walk backwards as he calls his chant to the bidders, finds himself getting confused. The man I was following was apparently new on the job. A group of poker-faced farmers watched him closely as he passed. He tripped on a bunch of bright lemon tobacco leaves, lost his rhythm and missed a bid. The warehouseman noticed the error and signalled for the incantation to stop. The auctioneer wiped his brow:

"I really screwed that one up."

Tobacco hogsheads—Danville

The group of bidders retraced their steps and began again two piles back. The farmers were not impressed:

"New fella."

"Yep."

"H'll learn."

"M'be."

It's a gruelling pace, so fast that the clerk hardly has time to record the bid before the next one starts. Five hundred piles or baskets an hour is considered only average. A year of arduous farming is graded and sold in a few brief minutes. A good auctioneer is a prominent citizen of the town. "Spec" Edwards, Bud Chandler, Bob Cage and Joe Burnett are considered by many to be the best in the business. It takes a long time for a newcomer to make his mark and these men are revered as artists by their followers. Some in addition to perfecting the bidding incantations also manage to add the human touch to auctions. In all that jumble of words there may occasionally be something to the effect that "Bob's had a bad year, help him out boys" or "Dick's son's going to college so let's give him a good send-off." Outsiders would never spot such references but the bidders always do, and usually cooperate by upping the deal a few cents a pound.

Many farmers prefer not to watch the auction process and gather around the coffee machines near the mini-bank that opens in the warehouse for each day's auction. I chatted with one old man, obviously disgruntled by the low price bid for his tobacco:

"Might as well sell it to't gover'm't" (there's a support price for each grade, offered by the federal government). "Hell, I'm not makin' a cent out'a this one. Same las' year and the year afore that one."

At midday the auction pauses. There's a break for lunch and much of the tobacco is prepared for dispatch to the redrying and storage warehouses where it is kept in thousand pound hogsheads until matured for production. I made the short trip to downtown Danville and explored the old hogshead warehouses by the river. There are some splendid pieces of urban architecture here, set off cobble streets. The area smells richly of tobacco. Bright yellow leaves lie scattered on the sidewalks and blow down the quiet streets. There's a tobacco museum too, housed in an old warehouse, with a comprehensive exhibit of every facet of the tobacco industry. If you take the guided tour, it could be more than an hour before you emerge, saturated with information. It's a favorite place for collectors of all types. The museum's displays of cigarette packets, cards, lighters, snuff brands and pipes are among the most valuable in the country.

While many of the smaller towns in the region have their tobacco auctions, none can compare with Danville, "Last Capital of the Confederacy." Below the fine

mansions on the bluff overlooking the Dan River, the town has a distinctly commercial character. Factories and warehouses fill the flatlands. Trucks snarl and grate up the steep grades, fast foods restaurants and chain motels line Route 58, Los Angeles-style, on the western side of town. It's not the kind of place a hidden-corner explorer would normally visit. However for those who wish to follow the tobacco trail through all its stages, Danville is a must.

The tobacco auctions begin during the month of August at ten or more warehouses in the town and continue until November. Usually, on any one day, there are four sales running concurrently and the public is welcome to attend each one.

The tobacco sold here is exclusively "Bright Leaf", the major type grown in Virginia, with more than 100 million pounds being produced annually. Bright leaf is the basic ingredient for cigarettes whereas "Burley" grown primarily in the southwest sector of the state (see "Abingdon and Vicinity") is particularly desirable for pipe tobacco and snuff. Other types include "Fire-Cured" used for snuff and chewing tobacco, and "Sun Cured" developed exclusively for plug chewing tobacco.

"Bright tobacco," grown on the often sparse soils of Piedmont in the south-central counties, is flue-cured by the farmers prior to market. Leave Danville and travel eastwards into the rugged rolling farmlands around South Boston, Kenbridge, Farmville and Keysville. This is real tobacco country. Take backroads at random. Some are just unpaved tracks leading through beautiful woodlands. Small 4- to 6-acre farms are scattered throughout the countryside, each with unusual groupings of tall windowless sheds, grouted with red earth between the thick crudely-trimmed log walls. These are the flue-curing sheds. Row upon row of fresh-cut "pickings" are hung from the floor to the ceiling and dried in the stove-heated shed. The process is far faster than the air-curing system normally used for the Burley and "sun cured" types. If you have a chance, stop and chat with the farmers. After the harvest they have some spare time on their hands and many delight in describing the intricacies of tobacco growing. It is the most labor-demanding of all field crops. In Virginia more than 50,000 farm families are involved in the process with seasonal immigrations for the harvest. Many of the families are black and live in tenant homes on the land, or nearby off the dusty tracks that criss-cross the back country. The landowners are normally white and the occasional modern ranch-style home set on a carefully mown lawn among garden bushes and flower-beds contrasts harshly with the living conditions of the tenants. However there seems to be a general acceptance of the status quo down here. I spoke to a motel-owner near Farmville: "It's always been this way. Used to be much worse in some counties. Nobody gets very rich growing tobacco on 6 acres and that's all that most folks 'round here have. I sometimes wonder why many of 'em bother to stay. They could likely make much more if they moved to Richmond or one o' those places."

But the heritage is strong. After all, tobacco was and still is a staple crop of Virginia. Back in the colonial days it was the only significant product of the region and was valued so highly that it was often used as a substitute for cash.

But opinions regarding the ethics of tobacco culture and consumption clashed fiercely. James I of England describes its usage as "a custom loathsome to the eye, hateful to the nose, harmful to the brain, dangerous to the lungs—in the black stinking fume thereof nearest resembling the horrible stygian smoke of the pit that is bottomless." Charles Kingsley, author of *Westward Ho!,* held very different views: "It is a lone man's companion, a bachelor's friend, a hungry man's food, a sad man's cordial, a wakeful man's sleep and a chilly man's fire . . . there is no herb like unto it, under the canopy of heaven."

Of course the same conflicts occur today. Anti-smoking organizations regale the public with threats, warnings and promises of grisly deaths while industry figures, particularly for cigarette production at nearby Richmond and Petersburg, tend to suggest a disheartening lack of impact of such campaigns. Tobacco continues to flourish and during late summer the mellow aromas of curing tobacco waft over the Piedmont and the tall chimneys of flue-barns send out tell-tale skimmers of warm air. Little seems to have changed. Although the slave-system has long been abolished, most of the tenant families have few alternatives but to continue their back-breaking labor in the tobacco fields.

Many of the towns reflect a bygone era. On the outskirts of Halifax is a magnificent line of palatial homes set in open estates, dotted with mature shade trees, and at nearby South Boston, groups of richly detailed Victorian mansions sit on the bluff overlooking the huddle of tobacco warehouses down by the railroad. But few places can match the charm of Charlotte Court House, south of Farmville, in the heart of tobacco country. It was here in 1799 that Patrick Henry and John Randolph of Roanoke matched wits in a famous debate that is re-staged by villagers on important occasions and holidays. Time seems to have passed the little town by. The 1823 courthouse with its thick white columns broods at the crossroads. Inside on its brick floor are display cases enclosing local historic artifacts and just down the road is the town museum set behind a white fence. During my last visit a group of wasps were setting up home on the gate, so I entered the back way via the library garden.

The gentleness of the surrounding scenery is apparently misleading. Pinned to the door of the courthouse here were detailed instructions on procedures to be followed after shooting bears in the county!

I love to wander this countryside, bears or no bears. It has all the easy feel of the deep south. Small country stores doze by the roadside. Paint-chipped rocking chairs creak in the shade of trelliced verandahs, a group of good ole boys sip beer down by the creek and children chase one another under the large trees on the village green.

There are also abundant parks and recreation areas scattered throughout the region. Not far to the east of South Boston is Buggs Island Lake and the Occoneechee State Park with beaches, boat launching ramps, picnic grounds and campsites. This is just one of dozens of recreation centers along the eight hundred miles of lake shoreline, but it's particularly interesting because of its links with Virginia's Indian culture. An island here, now submerged, used to be a center for the Occoneechee tribe and an important fur trading post until Nat Bacon and his militia (see "Northern Neck") destroyed the village and many of its occupants in 1676 during one of his forays against the Indians.

To the north there's a second charming recreation area at Goodwin Lake and the Prince Edward State Park. To the northwest is Holiday Lake State Park just outside historic Appomattox, site of the Confederacy surrender.

Of course, the region is also noted for its old plantations, a few of which have been preserved as authentic museums of the ante-bellum era. Haw Branch plantation, famous for its ghostly occurrences, is located a few miles north of Amelia just off Route 360 near Richmond. At South Boston there's the Little Plantation. Although less elaborate than most, the complex of buildings, which includes the main house, smoke house, carriage house, doctor's office, blacksmith shop and spring house, present a convincing portrayal of nineteenth century life on one of the smaller farms in the tobacco belt.

Further to the south, just over the border near Reidsville, North Carolina, is the Chinqua-Penn Plantation House. Built in the 1920s this is no plantation in the traditional sense of the word. It was in fact the home of tobacco magnate Thomas Jefferson Penn and his wife Beatrice, who used their fortune to surround them-

Verandah scene

selves with an extravagant collection of furnishings, art works and priceless religious objects. It's worth a visit if only to confirm the fact that not all those individuals connected with the tobacco industry find themselves grubbing over 6-acre small holdings.

Finally, in complete contrast, visit the Red Hill Shrine near Brookneal, Virginia. This was Patrick Henry's favorite home. He came here in 1796 intending to "plague myself no more with business, sitting down with what I have." The famous "give me liberty or give me death" orator, five times Virginia's chief executive, died and was buried here shortly after his debate at Charlotte Court House in 1799. He called this part of Virginia "the most tranquil place I have ever known."

I know what he meant.

INDEX